HOW TO BUILD AN AGENT

THE LEADER'S PLAYBOOK FOR CODING AND DEPLOYING AI THAT DELIVERS TANGIBLE BUSINESS RESULTS

KIERAN GILMURRAY

Across every major industry, interest in Agentic AI is growing at remarkable speed. It is one of the most discussed and least understood areas of artificial intelligence. Leaders hear the term constantly, yet many still ask what it actually means and how it will impact their organisation, their team, and their own role.

Technology has disrupted work before. The arrival of computers, the internet, and mobile reshaped entire economies. Nearly seventy percent of today's jobs did not exist a century ago. AI is now travelling along the same curve, but with a far steeper trajectory. Organisations are racing to embed AI and Generative AI in their operations, and Agentic AI is emerging as the next essential capability shaping industries and careers.

Why this book and why now

Recent surveys show that ninety percent of US IT executives believe their processes would benefit from Agentic AI. Thirty seven percent are already using it, and another thirty two percent are planning to invest. The timing could not be more important.

Some describe Agentic AI as a revolution. I prefer to treat it as a clear evolution. Yet it is an evolution that will have a much deeper impact on work and society than any AI seen so far.

The reason is simple. Agentic AI does not just execute a command. It can think, plan, act, and adapt. It can collaborate with people and other AI systems across networks and platforms. This creates a new model of work in which autonomous digital workers handle complex tasks that previously required trained humans.

Organisations that master this shift will improve efficiency, increase agility, and scale without the traditional limits of headcount. In many cases, agents will enhance the workforce by solving problems independently and completing sequences of interconnected tasks that move across systems. In other cases, agents will replace certain forms of labour entirely. People will need to focus on roles that involve complex judgment, creativity, care, innovation, and work where humanity adds irreplaceable value.

This is already happening. Industries are beginning to reorganise around teams that combine human expertise with autonomous AI systems that can anticipate needs, negotiate outcomes, and generate value without waiting for instruction. Agentic AI is not simply another technology trend. It is becoming a core driver of competitiveness.

Agentic AI will reshape business models, supply chains, decision making processes, labour structures, and executive responsibilities. Organisations that move early will gain a strategic advantage. Those that hesitate will find it increasingly difficult to compete in an economy shaped by intelligent automation.

The implications extend far beyond organisations. Workers, educators, policymakers, and governments will all need to adapt.

Why?

Agentic AI does not just execute tasks. It thinks, plans, actions, and adapts. Agents can also collaborate with each other and people across computer systems and networks, reshaping and transforming how work gets done.

In many instances, AI agents will enhance workforce capabilities by autonomously solving problems and completing complex tasks. For example, organizations that integrate autonomous agents effectively will unlock new levels of efficiency, agility, and intelligent decision-making, enabling them to scale operations without the traditional constraints of human resource capacity.

Yet increasingly, rather than assisting humans, as agents get smarter, they will increasingly replace human labor. Workers will need to focus on roles such as caregivers or those that involve AI technology, creative destruction, innovation, or other similar, non-AI, repeatable, high-value tasks to remain relevant. In the future, digital labor will become an indispensable strategic asset, complementing and, often, replacing human expertise, enabling business owners to create new business models.

This is not a distant projection; industries are already being redefined by agents. As ever, the challenge for leaders is not just adopting these technologies but reimagining how organizations operate in a world where AI-driven systems can anticipate needs, negotiate deals, and create value independently of people, just like you and me. Agentic AI is not just yet another tech trend. Its impact on business will be profound.

AI agents will not just automate tasks but fundamentally reshape business models, supply chains, decision-making processes, and labor markets and models. Organizations that harness this shift will gain a strategic advantage, while those that hesitate may struggle to compete in an economy increasingly driven by intelligent automation.

This change has huge implications for workers, governments, educators, and workers everywhere.

Who is this book for?

This book is written for managers, executives, consultants, entrepreneurs, and leaders who want clear, practical guidance on how to use AI to drive growth and innovation. It is not written for engineers. It is written for decision makers who must understand how autonomous systems will redefine competitive advantage and how to lead this shift with confidence.

Adopting AI is no longer the challenge. Leading AI is.

To do this well, leaders must understand the capabilities and limits of Agentic AI and learn how to apply it in ways that align with their organisation's goals and future strategy. This book will help you do exactly that.

What this books delivers

The book provides a structured, practical guide to understanding and implementing Agentic AI. It avoids hype and focuses on what leaders actually need. It offers actionable tools, including a business case template and a pilot programme charter, to help you start making informed decisions immediately.

It also provides a realistic and candid perspective on governance, risk, accountability, and the common reasons AI projects fail. By teaching leaders how to think about agentic strategy, it provides a long term mental model that will remain relevant as platforms and tools evolve.

The wider shift underway

We are now experiencing the most significant platform transition since the mobile revolution reshaped entire markets more than fifteen years ago. As mobile first companies captured disproportionate market share, new agent first companies will define the next decade.

Almost every organisation has added some form of generative AI to its stack. Yet most report little or no financial return. McKinsey calls this the gen AI paradox. The pattern is familiar. Companies adopt a new technology quickly to avoid falling behind, but struggle to monetise it.

The most credible way out of the paradox is through autonomous agents. These systems are not chatbots sitting on a website. They are embedded inside business processes and allowed to take action. This requires clarity about goals, workflows, and incentives long before money is spent on tools.

The shift is already creating a divide. Some organisations are building early capability, knowing that the value compounds over time as agents generate data, improve, and unlock more ambitious use cases. Others are falling behind.

A clear distinction: agents and chatbots

A traditional chatbot answers questions. An AI agent can act. It can hold context, use memory, execute multi step workflows, and work across systems.

A modern agent can speak to a customer, validate a payment, run fraud checks, resolve a billing issue, reprocess a shipment, update the CRM, and notify the team. This move from reactive systems to proactive digital workers is where competitive advantage now emerges.

If the past two years were the equivalent of the iPhone launch, the next five years will mirror the rise of the App Store. The real transformation begins when thousands of new workflows are built, tested, and refined.

By 2028, agents will not simply write content or book meetings. They will collaborate in clusters. One agent will scan the market and detect emerging topics. Another will generate the first version of an article. A third will create visual assets. A fourth will orchestrate the project and deliver the final output. Humans will review the work rather than complete the steps.

Research from Deloitte confirms that the value lies in entire workflows, not isolated tasks.

Organisations that begin building these muscles now will be far ahead of those that wait.

Real world results

McKinsey's recent research shows measurable gains where agents are used effectively.

- Customer satisfaction rises sharply. Up to eighty percent of common service incidents can be resolved autonomously.
- Cost reduction increases as repetitive and error prone work is automated.
- Process times fall by sixty to ninety percent where workflows are redesigned for agent autonomy.

These benefits are yours to capture if you start now and build the capability before your competitors do.

Enjoy,

Kieran

WHO IS KIERAN GILMURRAY?

Kieran Gilmurray MBA (1st). MSc. PG Dip. Teaching. BSc. (Hons) Management Science

Kieran Gilmurray is an author, industry analyst, real-world business technology transformation strategist, and implementer. He is an internationally renowned expert in AI, automation, data analytics, and digital transformation. Kieran has over 30 years of experience developing innovative digital transformation solutions tailored to medium, large, and global-scale organizations.

He is recognized for his ability to deliver actionable strategies that enable organizations to adapt and thrive in the digital world. Kieran's work has generated more than $300 million of value for organizations to date. His experience working with global enterprises in leadership and organizational development, automation, AI, blockchain, data, and cloud makes him a unique and highly sought-after consultant and advisor.

Kieran regularly delivers conference keynotes worldwide and appears on stage in front of some of the world's largest organizations. He is consistently ranked as one of the top global experts in Artificial Intelligence, Intelligent Automation, data analytics, brand influence, and business technology innovation.

He has received multiple international awards, including being named to prestigious lists such as the Top 50 Global Thought Leader and Influencer on Agentic AI and Generative AI, a Best LinkedIn Influencer for AI and Marketing, a Global Intelligent Automation Award Winner, a Top 50 Global Thought Leaders and Influencers on Manufacturing, a seven time Linkedin Top Voice, Top 14 people to follow in data and one of the World's Top 200 Business and Technology Innovators.

His leadership roles for FTSE 100 organizations have focused on global artificial intelligence, intelligent automation, and technology business management, both as a strategist and an implementer. Kieran's expertise extends to building global intelligent automation centers of high and emerging technologies, significantly enhancing productivity, profitability, and overall business performance.

When he is not chairing international conferences or delivering masterclasses to industry leaders, he is actively consulting for leading global organizations, driving AI, automation, digital transformation, and innovation programs.

To stay updated on the latest trends in business technology, follow Kieran on his company's website: kierangilmurray.com or connect with him on LinkedIn, Spotify, YouTube, or X (formerly Twitter).

Kieran Gilmurray

MBA MSc PG Dip. BSc (Hons)

CEO of Kieran Gilmurray and Company Limited,
a global technology consulting firm.

CONTENTS

Introduction — 11

CHAPTER 1.
The Platform Shift Creating New Market Leaders — 13

CHAPTER 2.
The Executive's Framework for Agent Strategy — 21

CHAPTER 3.
The New Agentic Organization: People, Processes, and Platforms — 31

CHAPTER 4.
Your Minimum Viable Toolchain & "Hello, World!" AI Agent — 43

CHAPTER 5.
From Single Tasks to Workflows — 55

CHAPTER 6.
Giving Your Agent Memory (The Knowledge Agent) — 71

CHAPTER 7.
From Single Agent to Swarm — 83

CHAPTER 8.
Architecture That Scales — 93

CHAPTER 9.
Governance, Guardrails, and Ethics — 103

CHAPTER 10.
Measuring Success — ROI That Matters to the Board — 115

CHAPTER 11.
The Build vs. Buy Decision Framework — 127

CHAPTER 12.
Your First 4-Week Pilot Program — 141

CHAPTER 13.
Your Personalized AI Implementation Roadmap — 153

CHAPTER 14.
The Future of Agentic Systems — 167

Appendix A: The Agentic Readiness Assessment (ARA) Worksheet 177
Appendix B: One-Page Business Case Template 183
Appendix C: AI Pilot Program Charter Template 185
Appendix D: Sample Job Descriptions for Key Agentic Roles 189
Glossary of Terms 195

INTRODUCTION

How to Read this book

This book should be read sequentially, which is legitimate for the task at hand.

That is because what you're holding in your hand is a manual designed to help the non-specialist line-of-business manager, intrigued and inspired by all the current talk of Agentic AI, start building autonomous agents in their own organizations.

Agentic AI's benefits, which are real, do not come just from flicking a switch on a software robot or two in your accounts payable department. The reality is that there is a significant margin for error here. Wasted costs from poorly imaged or implemented Agentic AI programs can be significant.

I authored this book to try and stop that from happening.

What I want to do is to make it easier for people like you to make sense of agentic AI. Written to help clear some of the fog, it is the result of my own years of experience helping customers like you achieve long-lasting positive results with IT.

I hope that this book will help you and your organization become more successful by utilizing this wonderful technology.

Kieran Gilmurray

Agentic AI, Artificial Intelligence, Digital Transformation, and Data Analytics Consultant Director

CHAPTER 1

The Platform Shift Creating New Market Leaders

The business world is experiencing its most significant platform shift since the mobile telephone revolution disrupted entire industries over fifteen years ago. Just as companies that embraced mobile-first strategies captured disproportionate market share, while legacy players scrambled to catch up, we're now witnessing the emergence of the "agentic economy".

Almost every company (80%) has incorporated generative AI somewhere into its technology stack. And nearly every one of those companies (80%) says it hasn't impacted their bottom line. McKinsey calls this the "gen AI paradox". It is just the usual story of new technology: everyone rushes to adopt it because they're afraid of being left behind, but they don't know how to monetise it.

The way out of the paradox is "autonomous agents." Not just chatbots duct-taped onto a help page, but actual systems embedded in the organizational bloodstream, allowed to do things on their own. That sounds cool in theory, but in practice, it requires the one thing corporations struggle with: thinking clearly about their goals, processes, structures, and incentives before investing money in technology.

So, we're at another inflection point. Either companies figure out how to deploy agents in a way that's as transformative as mobile-first was for Apple and Google, or they will end up as the next Blackberry and Nokia, remembered mostly in business school case studies and "Where Are They Now?" slides.

AI Agents vs. Chatbots: Proactive vs. Reactive Systems

Understanding the distinction between AI agents and chatbots is crucial if your goal is to achieve digital transformation in business operations. Chatbots respond to specific queries and, if they are integrated with an LLM-based API, they can then generate unique and relevant content in response to prompts.

AI agents operate with autonomy, memory, and the ability to execute complex workflows across multiple computer systems.

Today, an agent can communicate with the customer, confirm that their payment was successful, verify for potential fraud, resolve a customer's billing issue, reprocess a shipment, and then log all of this information in the CRM.

This shift from reactive to proactive, i.e., from answering to acting, is exactly where competitive advantage now lies.

The leap from chatbots to agents comes from four capabilities:

Memory Systems: Unlike the amnesiac chatbot, an agent remembers the last conversation, the last action, and the last outcome, building a stateful representation of the user interaction or process workflow.

Reasoning Capabilities: Agents can break down complex business challenges into component parts, examine the relationships between those parts, and then create and execute effective strategies to address them.

Integration Power: Like an API cyborg, an agent embeds itself as a nervous system across your company's software, allowing it to coordinate actions between previously siloed corporate organs such as CRM, ERP, and email.

Autonomous Execution: Perhaps most critically, agents can take action without constant human prompting. This will eventually eliminate the need for many of the middle management's current tasks, which is a big business advantage.

The Agentic Loop

Agents operate on a four-stage cycle, called the "Agent Loop". This loop may also be referred to by other names, such as the **Perceive-Reason-Act** cycle or the **Thought-Action-Observation** cycle.

Perceive: The agent takes in data from its environment. Not just a user's text query but a constant stream of information. It could be a real-time feed of market data, usage logs from your CRM, new support tickets, or an urgent email from a key client. Through all this input, the agent builds a high-res map of its assigned domain.

Think: The agent analyzes the data it has perceived, breaks down its high-level goal into executable steps, and decides which tools it needs to use. For instance, an agent would ask to "schedule a meeting with the sales team to discuss the Q3 forecast." They would first find a mutual opening on everyone's calendar, then search the shared drive for the relevant forecast document, and finally schedule the meeting with the updated Q3 forecast document attached.

Act: The agent executes the plan by connecting to other systems via APIs. For example, by logging into a CRM, drafting an email, booking a meeting, etc. Here, you have the choice of having a human-in-the-loop to validate and check the agent's actions or letting it do these things autonomously.

Learn: The agent observes the outcome of its actions and integrates this feedback into its memory, refining its strategies over time. For example, it can learn which outreach messages are most effective and which customer behavior patterns are the true predictors of churn, among other things.

The Growth Wave: What to Expect from 2026-2030

If 2024-2025 is the "iPhone moment," then the period from 2026 to 2030 will be akin to the "App Store explosion."

The real action starts not when the tool exists, but when a million experiments begin to stack on top of it. The first wave of agent adoption is mostly about *novelty and tinkering*: you give people a tool, they try it, they collect data. The data feeds back into the system, the system improves, and then *that* improvement feeds back into the users, who generate more ambitious use cases, which in turn feed more data back into the system... and so forth.

By 2028, it won't just be "your agent books your meetings" or "your agent writes SEO content."

A lone agent today might already draft a blog post. The agent hives of 2028 will autonomously manage the entire action sequence: one agent continuously monitors search trends and news for new and emerging topics; a second agent, with a different 'personality' tuned for virality, drafts the first first written piece; a third generates a suite of complementary visual and social assets; a fourth acts like the project manager who makes sure the other three executives and then presents the final result to a designated human.

As Deloitte has commented, the real value of AI is found in redesigning work to integrate humans and machines within entire workflows. This is where the real value lies: not in isolated 'prompted toy tasks' but in entire workflows stitched together, with humans increasingly acting more as reviewers and orchestrators.

If this model holds, the companies that built their muscles early (in 2025–2026), when everyone else was still deciding whether agents were "a fad", will dominate ahead. They'll already have the datasets and institutional know-how to iteratively refine their agentic infrastructure – but you won't if you haven't even started.

Companies Using Agents Seeing Dramatic Improvements

Recent research by McKinsey reveals that companies successfully deploying AI agents are seeing substantial improvements:

- **Customer Satisfaction Enhancement**: McKinsey reports that up to 80% of common service incidents can be resolved autonomously.
- **Operational Cost Reduction**: Early case studies show that AI agents can streamline repetitive, error-prone tasks and improve overall productivity. In one study, generative AI improved issue resolution by 14% per hour for customer service agents, thereby reducing handling times and enabling them to focus on more complex cases that truly required their time and attention.

- **Process Acceleration**: In scenarios where workflows have been fully reimagined with agent autonomy, McKinsey estimates that end-to-end process times can drop by 60–90%, since autonomous agents eliminate delays from human handoffs and execute activities in parallel.

These results are not just theoretical. They are most visible in organizations that are moving beyond pilot projects toward the deeper integration of agentic AI into core operations.

The "Agent Economy": New Business Models and Revenue Streams Opening Up

Sometimes, technologies don't just make existing things faster; they change what "things" are. Cars weren't just faster horses; they were the start of suburbs, road trips, drive-throughs, and traffic jams.

Smartphones weren't just smaller computers; they were Uber, Tinder, food delivery apps, PayPal, and the dopamine economy of infinite scroll.

Agent-as-a-Service Models: Build an agent, sell it. OpenAI now enables companies like Stripe and Box to create custom business agents and monetize them as APIs. Consider: a bank's internal risk-scoring system is transformed into a product that outsiders can rent, generating a new income stream for the bank.

Autonomous Business Processes: Agents can handle complete workflows independently. Real estate agents (the digital kind!) can identify opportunities, conduct market analysis, and even manage early negotiations. For instance, DHL runs AI agents that optimize routes, manage warehouses, forecast demand, and reduce travel distance.

Embedded Intelligence Revenue: Products gain autonomous capabilities. Agricultural equipment schedules its own maintenance based on usage patterns and weather forecasts. Companies like Siemens and GE use embedded AI agents to monitor turbines, jet engines, and factory equipment. Software applications adapt their interfaces and functionality to individual users over time. Enabling companies to react with more agility, intelligence, and impact than their competition.

Dynamic Pricing and Personalization: Agents can personalize beyond recommendations. E-commerce platforms adjust pricing, product placement, and promotional offers in real-time based on individual customer behavior, inventory levels, and competitive positioning.

There is huge economic potential. Industry analysts project the AI agent market will reach $50 billion by 2027, but this figure likely underestimates the broader economic transformation as agents become embedded throughout business ecosystems.

Competitive Risk

History provides clear precedent for what happens during platform transitions. When mobile computing emerged, companies faced a critical choice: to embrace the new platform early and risk short-term costs and complexity, or wait for the technology to mature and risk being displaced competitively. The winners were decisive. Apple didn't wait for mobile technology to be perfect before launching the iPhone. They bet on the platform's trajectory and captured disproportionate value as the ecosystem developed. Similarly, companies like Uber, Airbnb, and Instagram built their entire business models around mobile capabilities that established players dismissed as immature or niche.

Today's AI agent adoption follows similar patterns. Early movers are not waiting for perfect technology. They're building competitive advantages while their competitors debate implementation timelines. The risks of waiting compound daily:

First-Mover Advantage: Companies that deploy agents now are building institutional knowledge, refining processes, and developing agent-optimised workflows that will be difficult for competitors to replicate.. They're also establishing relationships with key technology partners and securing top AI talent before the market becomes saturated.

Data Network Effects: Agents depend on the quality and accessibility of enterprise data. Organizations that begin integrating agents immediately start reaping the benefits of data network effects. As agents process more information, they become more effective, creating a self-reinforcing competitive advantage.

Customer Experience Moats: Companies that utilize agents to deliver superior customer experiences are elevating customer expectations across the industry. Competitors offering traditional service models appear increasingly outdated by comparison, making it progressively harder to win new customers or retain existing ones..

Operational Efficiency Gaps: Organizations that achieve cost reductions through agent deployment can reinvest those savings in further innovation, marketing, or competitive pricing strategies. Thus, creating compounding advantages over competitors who still operate with manual processes.

Talent and Partnership Access: The ecosystem of agent-capable developers, consultants, and technology partners is still in its early stages of development.

Early movers have preferential access to the best resources, while later adopters face increasingly competitive talent markets and longer implementation queues.

Concluding Thoughts

The mobile platform shift created trillion-dollar companies and obsoleted entire business models within a decade. The agent platform shift is following a similar trajectory, but with compressed timelines and amplified impact. The window for establishing first-mover advantage is now measured in months, not years, and shrinking.

The platform shift is underway. Will your company be among the agents of change or among the casualties of transformation?

References:

- https://www.deloitte.com/us/en/about/press-room/work-design-essential-to-ai-roi.html
- https://www.dhl.com/discover/en-ae/logistics-advice/logistics-insights/ai-in-logistics-and-last-mile-delivery
- https://www.mckinsey.com/capabilities/quantumblack/our-insights/seizing-the-agentic-ai-advantage

CHAPTER 2

The Executive's Framework for Agent Strategy

The most successful technology transformations in business history have been led by executives who focused on core business principles. Steve Jobs didn't need to be a chip designer to envision the iPhone. Jeff Bezos didn't need to be a database engineer to architect Amazon's marketplace. Similarly, executives don't need to understand the intricacies of neural networks to make strategic decisions about AI agents. That said, they do need a clear mental model as to what agents can do and how they create value.

You'd never hire someone without knowing what they're good at. So don't deploy AI agents without understanding their architecture.

In this chapter, we'll look at how to think strategically about agents and what makes them different from regular software.

Memory in Modern AI Systems

What is the single greatest limitation of early AI models, such as GPT-1? It forgot everything - true digital amnesia. They gave brilliant answers—then instantly forgot the conversation. For business, that was unacceptable. You cannot help a customer if you lose their name and problem in seconds. Newer models fixed this flaw.

Short-term or working memory is what enables modern AI to maintain conversational continuity. Rather than treating each interaction as a blank slate, the system uses a dynamic context window to capture recent exchanges, user instructions, and reasoning steps. This enables the AI to track conversations, resolve ambiguities, and respond in a coherent manner. Working memory acts like a scratchpad, holding just enough information for the current task but fading once the task ends unless it is stored in a longer-term system.

Episodic Memory and Retrieval Augmentation Generation (RAG)

A further challenge arises when a question requires information that was either missing from the training dataset or generated after the model's knowledge cut-off. In such cases, an LLM may hallucinate - producing factually incorrect outputs - or default to a generic response such as 'this is outside my capabilities'.

Retrieval-Augmented Generation (RAG) is a powerful technique that enhances an LLM's response by grounding it in external, up-to-date information. This type of memory is often referred to as episodic memory. When a user submits a query, the system does not rely only on its pre-trained data. Instead, it first searches a defined corpus, such as internal documents, spreadsheets, or wikis, before generating an answer. This ensures outputs are both contextually relevant and factually supported.

Step-by-Step RAG Example

Let's imagine you are working at a company, and you want to use an internal chatbot to ask a question about the company's policy regarding the use of a personal laptop for work purposes.

Step 0: The Query

You start by typing your question into the company's AI chatbot:

"Can I use my personal laptop for work projects?"

This query is sent to the Large Language Model (LLM). Without RAG, the LLM would have to guess the answer based on its general, pre-existing training data, which more likely than not does not include your specific company's IT policies.

Step 1: Retrieval (The "R" in RAG)

The system searches a specific collection of documents, which in this case is your company's internal knowledge base. This includes documents such as an "IT Security Policy PDF," an "Employee Handbook," or internal wiki pages regarding the use of personal IT equipment.

- **Semantic Search with Vector Embeddings:** This is not a simple keyword search. The RAG system converts your query and all company documents into numerical representations known as vector embeddings. These vectors capture the *meaning* of the text. The system now looks for documents whose meaning is mathematically closest to the meaning of your query.
- **Finding Relevant Information:** Because it's searching by meaning, it might find a section in the IT Security document titled *"Policy on Use of Non-Company Devices"* and another in the onboarding guide called *"Bring Your Own Device (BYOD) Guidelines."* Even though these don't contain the exact phrase "personal laptop," they are semantically relevant.

Step 2: Augmenting the Prompt (The "A" in RAG)

The system now combines the relevant snippets of text it found with your original question. This is known as the Augmentation phase.

The simple prompt is transformed into a much more detailed and context-rich prompt that is then passed to the LLM. It looks something like this:

Context:

- From IT Security Policy: *"Use of personal devices to access company data is permitted only if the device is enrolled in the company's Mobile Device Management (MDM) software and passes a security compliance check."*
- From BYOD Guidelines: *"Employees who choose to use personal laptops for work are eligible for a monthly stipend of $50 but must ensure all company-related work is stored exclusively on the company's secure cloud drive, not the local machine."*

Original Question:
"Can I use my personal laptop for work projects?"

Instruction:
"Using only the context provided above, answer the user's question."

Step 3: Generating the Final Answer (The "G" in RAG)

Finally, the LLM receives this augmented prompt. This is the **Generation** phase.

Grounded by the specific, factual information from your company's documents, the model can now generate a precise and helpful answer, rather than a generic or incorrect one.

The chatbot's final response to you would be:

"Yes, you can use your personal laptop for work, provided it is enrolled in our MDM software. You will also be eligible for a $50 monthly stipend, but you must store all company work on our secure cloud drive."

By following these steps, RAG ensures the model's answer is not just a guess, but is based on actual, verifiable data from a trusted source.

Traditional RAG vs Agentic RAG

Everything described above - retrieving relevant documents, augmenting the prompt, and generating a grounded response - is what we call *traditional RAG*. In traditional RAG, the system typically retrieves context from a fixed, single source in a one-shot process, then uses that information to generate an answer.

Agentic RAG extends this approach by embedding autonomous agents. These agents can dynamically decide which tools or data sources to query, switch between multiple databases, and reformulate questions if the initial retrieval is insufficient. Agents may also perform iterative searches or ask for clarification, introducing adaptability and multi-step reasoning into the process.

Fine-Tuning and Semantic Memory

Fine-tuning is a method that adapts a pre-trained LLM to a specific domain by continuing its training with a high-quality, domain-specific dataset. For instance, fine-tuning a model on thousands of technical support queries enables it to recognize the patterns and solutions typical of that context.

During this process, the model's internal parameters, also known as "weights," are adjusted through a technique called backpropagation. In doing so, the model develops domain expertise and a more refined reasoning process. It reshapes the model's internal parameters to align its reasoning process with a specialized task.

Think of RAG as like giving someone a library of medical textbooks: the knowledge is available, but it must be looked up each time. Fine-tuning is like sending that person to medical school. After training, a doctor carries an ingrained, intuitive understanding of how symptoms and systems connect without needing to consult a book for every case.

Memory Systems: Why Agents That "Remember" Drive Higher Customer Lifetime Value

The memory capabilities of AI agents represent one of their most significant business advantages. Unlike traditional software, which operates statelessly and treats each interaction as a fresh start, agents can maintain persistent, searchable memory across engagements, building and compounding value over time.

From a business standpoint, this memory architecture delivers three critical outcomes:

1. **Escalating Value**: Each interaction enhances the agent's effectiveness for future use, creating a compounding cycle of performance gains that traditional software cannot match.
2. **Personalization at Scale**: Agents deliver individually customized experiences without the typical costs associated with personalization, enabling mass customization across large customer bases.
3. **Institutional Knowledge**: Agent memory becomes a persistent repository of organizational learning, thereby reducing knowledge loss due to employee turnover and enabling the continuous optimization of processes.

Prompt Engineering

Prompt engineering is the practice of carefully and deliberately shaping inputs to guide an LLM toward a desired output. Unlike RAG and fine-tuning, this approach does not alter the model's architecture or require new data. Instead, it draws on the model's existing capabilities by structuring the prompt in a way that activates the most relevant patterns learned during its initial training.

At its simplest, prompt engineering involves refining a vague query into one that is sufficiently clear and detailed.

For example:

- **Poorly Written Prompt:** *"Is this code secure?"*
- **Well-Engineered Prompt:** *"Review the following Python code for potential security vulnerabilities, including input validation, authentication, and data handling. List any issues you find, explain why they are risks, and suggest safer alternatives."*

More advanced prompt engineering techniques include embedding examples, supplying additional context, or specifying explicit formatting requirements. These methods enable greater precision, consistency, and control over model outputs.

For example, an effective prompt for a business agent might include:

- **Persona** – *"You are a helpful and professional customer support agent for our company."*
- **High-Level Goal** – *"Your primary objective is to resolve customer issues quickly and accurately."*
- **Available Tools** – *"You have access to the following tools: a knowledge base search, a CRM lookup, and a ticket escalation tool."*
- **Constraints and Guardrails** – *"You must never provide medical or legal advice. If a customer expresses frustration, you must immediately escalate their ticket to a human manager."*

Crafting prompts of this kind is now an essential business skill. The clarity and precision of your instructions directly shape the quality, reliability, and safety of an agent's performance.

RAG vs Fine Tuning vs Prompt Engineering

Each method serves a distinct purpose in shaping how agents perform.

- **Retrieval-Augmented Generation (RAG):** Best suited for providing agents with access to up-to-date or organization-specific information, functioning as episodic memory. Its drawbacks include latency from the retrieval step and added costs for storing and processing external corpora.
- **Fine-Tuning:** The primary method for instilling semantic memory, giving the model deep expertise in a domain. Fine-tuning integrates specialized knowledge directly into the model, resulting in faster inference since no retrieval is required. However, it is resource-intensive, requires ongoing retraining for updates, and carries the risk of catastrophic forgetting, where domain learning weakens general capabilities.
- **Prompt Engineering:** The most lightweight approach. It requires no changes to infrastructure, provides immediate feedback, and offers high flexibility. Its limitations are trial-and-error refinement and dependence on the model's existing knowledge base, without the addition of new information.

Rule of Thumb:

Start with prompt engineering to test performance. If accuracy remains insufficient, consider adding RAG or function calling to expand knowledge. If deeper specialization is needed, fine-tune the base model.

The ReAct and Perceive-Think-Act-Learn Loops

If memory provides an agent with knowledge, reasoning, and acting gives it the ability to pursue goals - breaking a large objective into a dynamic, step-by-step plan.

The most widely adopted approach today is ReAct, short for *Reason-and-Act*. In this model, the agent alternates between "thinking out loud" and taking action in a recurring cycle:

- **Reason**: The agent evaluates the current context and decides the next subtask.
- **Act**: It executes the necessary tool or action.
- **Observe**: It reviews the outcome, using that feedback to inform its next step in reasoning.

For example, when asked to schedule a meeting:

1. **Reason**: "I need team availability—check the calendar."
2. **Act**: Calls the calendar tool.
3. **Observe**: Receives availability data, then reasons again: "Q3 forecast doc needed - search files."
4. **Act**: Executes a document search.
5. **Repeat** until the goal is complete.

In most implementations, "observe" is not called out separately—it is folded into reasoning. After every action, the agent immediately processes the outcome, integrates it into its reasoning trace, and decides what to do next. As a result, the practical loop is: **Reason → Act → Reason → Act.**

Current frameworks such as LangChain, LangGraph, AutoGen, and CrewAI rely heavily on ReAct-style loops.

Perceive–Think–Act–Learn

The **Perceive–Think–Act–Learn** loop is a broader, older model drawn from robotics, cognitive science, and control systems.

It frames an **autonomous agent** as one that:

- **Perceives** its environment (sensors, data streams, user inputs)
- **Thinks** by planning or reasoning about possible actions)
- **Acts** by executing a decision in the real or digital environment
- **Learns** by adapting from outcomes, updating its model or behavior

This framework represents the longer-term vision for agentic AI: systems with situational awareness, adaptive learning, and persistent memory that enable continuous improvement and a sense of autonomy.

Reasoning Capabilities: How Agents Break Down Complex Business Processes

Agentic AI systems bring reasoning to automation. They can decompose tasks, leverage external tools such as web search or calculators, interact with humans, and even collaborate with other agents. This reasoning ability is transforming how organizations handle complex, multi-step workflows that once required extensive human coordination.

Decomposition: Agents break large objectives into manageable subtasks. For example, a directive to *"optimize customer onboarding"* becomes a structured sequence: analyze funnel performance, identify friction points, research best practices, propose improvements, test solutions, and measure outcomes.

Planning: Beyond simple task execution, agents design strategies that optimize for multiple objectives simultaneously. They can plan parallel workstreams, anticipate resource constraints, identify dependencies, and adapt sequences as priorities shift.

Exception Handling: Unlike rigid automation systems, agents can reason through unexpected situations and respond accordingly. Faced with an edge case, they evaluate alternatives, consult knowledge bases, escalate appropriately, and retain what they learn for future scenarios.

Cross-Domain Integration: Agents reason across organizational silos, weighing sales impact, inventory constraints, customer satisfaction, and financial implications at the same time. This provides holistic business insight traditionally associated with senior human judgment.

Integration: Tool Use to Connect to Existing Systems

Tool use is where an agent's intelligence connects with the real world of business. It transforms an agent from a closed "black box" into an active, integrated part of your digital ecosystem. In agentic terms, a "tool" is any system the agent can access through an API (Application Programming Interface) to perceive information or take action.

This is the most critical capability for executives to understand because it drives tangible ROI. Reasoning without integration delivers little value - agents must interact with the systems that run the enterprise.

API Integration: Agents connect directly with enterprise software through APIs. They can read data from CRM systems, update inventory platforms, trigger financial workflows, and coordinate across the technology stack without costly system replacements.

Tool Utilization: Agents interact with APIs, databases, search engines, and specialized applications to facilitate seamless integration. They can perform competitive web searches, run calculations for financial modeling, query customer databases, and activate workflows across multiple platforms.

Multi-System Orchestration: Acting as orchestration layers, agents coordinate workflows spanning multiple systems. For example, they can initiate a customer service request, check inventory, verify payment, arrange shipping, update CRM records, and trigger follow-up communication, all while maintaining full context.

Real-Time Adaptation: By integrating with live systems, agents make decisions based on current states rather than historical data. They can adjust recommendations to reflect real-time inventory, modify pricing in response to demand, or escalate issues using live performance metrics.

Conclusion

Agents are not magic. Their power comes from combining memory, planning, and tools into a deliberate methodology that solves real business challenges. As a leader, the task is not to be mystified by AI, but to architect the strategy that directs its capabilities.

CHAPTER 3

The New Agentic Organization: People, Processes, and Platforms

Why do ambitious technology projects collapse? Not because of weak code or cloud infrastructure. They fail because organizations don't adapt.

You can buy the most powerful AI model available. But if people aren't equipped, processes aren't redesigned, and leaders don't set the right tone, AI becomes shelfware: expensive, promising, unused.

Agentic AI raises the stakes. These aren't tools you plug in; they're co-workers. They change workflows, reshape roles, and challenge managers to think differently about how outcomes get delivered.

The winners don't treat this as "installing new software." They build a new operating model—where human creativity and machine intelligence operate in a seamless loop.

Today, nearly every business invests in AI. Yet only 1% reach maturity—where AI drives measurable outcomes across workflows. Their edge isn't technology. Its structure.

This chapter serves as your playbook for joining them.

Managing a Hybrid Workforce

For decades, management has meant directing people to perform tasks. The role resembled a factory foreman, monitoring output on the assembly line.

But in the agentic era, the metaphor shifts. Leaders are more like conductors of an orchestra—coordinating humans and AI agents, each with distinct strengths, to deliver harmony and results. Some of the most consistent and scalable "musicians" in that orchestra are now digital.

This shift from task management to outcome management matters. Task management focuses on controlling inputs—who does what, when, and how. Outcome management focuses on results—defining success and letting the optimal mix of human creativity and AI capability chart the path.

Key Leadership Capabilities for the Agentic Era

Outcome-Oriented Management: Great leaders set business goals and standards, then let hybrid teams decide how to achieve them. Instead of instructing, "generate 50 leads per week," outcome-driven leaders say, "grow the qualified pipeline by 15%." Humans build the strategy and focus on relationship building, AI agents scale research, outreach, and data analysis.

AI Literacy for Executives: Executives don't need to be machine learning experts. However, they must understand what agents can and cannot do—how memory

(RAG) extends knowledge, how reasoning (ReAct) enables problem-solving, and how tool use integrates with business processes. This literacy equips leaders to set realistic goals, ask the right questions, and make better strategic decisions.

Fostering Psychological Safety in Human-AI Teams: Working alongside AI is unsettling for many. Some humans will even take guidance from agents. Leaders must build cultures where experimentation is safe, agent recommendations are trusted, and corrections are not threatening. Position agents as collaborators, not replacements.

Risk-Aware Decision Making: Every deployment carries compliance, brand, and operational risks. Strong leaders don't freeze under risk; they strike a balance between speed and responsibility. They weigh regulation, brand impact, and continuity without stalling progress.

Redesigning the Organization

Traditional structures were designed for an era of information scarcity and human bottlenecks. Hierarchies and silos made sense when data was hard to gather and coordination was costly.

AI agents erase those constraints. They process vast amounts of information, coordinate instantly across functions, and make routine decisions autonomously. To unlock this, organizations need a fundamentally different architecture.

The Hub-and-Spoke Model: Your AI Center of Excellence

Many enterprises now experiment with AI Centers of Excellence (CoEs). In the U.S., up to 37% of large firms report having one. However, most operate as IT support units, rather than engines of strategic transformation.

The agentic organization requires a reimagined CoE—functioning as the **hub** of AI capability—with business units as **spokes** that tailor and scale agents to their specific needs.

The future organization looks more like a **hub-and-spoke system**:

- The **Hub** (AI CoE) drives strategy, develops shared agent capabilities, enforces governance, and upskills talent.
- The **Spokes** (business units) apply these capabilities in their domains, customize agents, monitor performance, and provide feedback to the hub.

The "Hub": Your Strategic AI Center of Excellence The Hub serves as the central nervous system for your organization's AI capabilities. Rather than simply managing technology, it orchestrates the strategic deployment of AI agents across the organization.

Hub Responsibilities:

- **Strategic AI Roadmap**: Identifying high-impact opportunities for agent deployment
- **Core Agent Development**: Building foundational AI capabilities that multiple business units can leverage
- **Governance and Risk Management**: Ensuring all agent deployments meet compliance, security, and brand standards
- **Performance Optimization**: Continuously improving agent effectiveness across the organization
- **Talent Development**: Building AI collaboration skills across the organization

The "Spokes": Business Unit Agent Deployment Each business unit functions as a spoke, identifying specific opportunities within its domain and deploying agents to solve targeted problems. Spokes maintain deep business expertise while leveraging Hub capabilities for technical implementation.

Spoke Responsibilities:

- **Opportunity Identification**: Finding specific use cases where agents can create business value
- **Agent Customization**: Tailoring Hub-developed capabilities to specific business needs
- **Performance Monitoring**: Measuring and reporting on agent effectiveness in their domain
- **User Training**: Ensuring their teams can work effectively with deployed agents
- **Feedback Loop**: Providing insights back to the Hub for strategic optimization

Together, this hub-and-spoke model ensures AI isn't confined to isolated projects but embedded across the business—scaling impact, sharing learning, and driving competitive advantage.

Visual Organization: Before and After

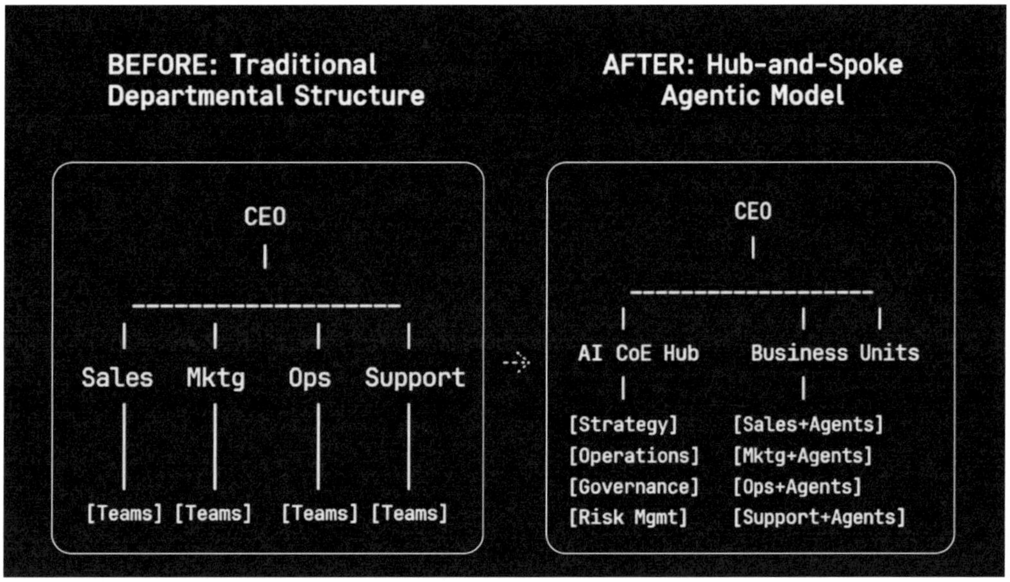

The key difference is that business units maintain their domain expertise while gaining AI capabilities through the Hub, creating hybrid human-AI teams that can accomplish far more than either could alone.

Defining the New Roles: Your Human-AI Team

An agentic organization requires roles that didn't exist five years ago. These positions bridge the gap between traditional business functions and AI capabilities, ensuring that technological power translates into business outcomes.

The Three Critical New Roles

The AI Agent Orchestrator ($95K-140K annually)

Role: The "Manager" of Your Agent Workforce

As organizations deploy AI agents at scale, a new leadership role emerges: the **Agent Orchestrator**. Much like traditional managers lead human teams, orchestrators guide fleets of AI systems. They set objectives, monitor performance, optimize workflows, and ensure that technology consistently advances business priorities. In doing so, they become the bridge between human judgment and machine execution.

Core Responsibilities:

- **Agent Performance Management**: Continuously monitoring effectiveness, identifying optimization opportunities, and ensuring output meets business standards.

- **Workflow Integration**: Embedding agents seamlessly into human teams so collaboration is natural, not disruptive.
- **Objective Setting**: Converting strategic goals into precise, measurable targets that AI systems can execute reliably.
- **Quality Assurance**: Maintaining consistency, accuracy, and compliance across agent-driven processes.
- **Escalation Management**: Taking ownership of exceptions and edge cases where human oversight is required.

Skills Profile:

Effective Orchestrators blend business process expertise, data literacy, project management discipline, and strong communication skills. They are able to manage both technical complexity and human alignment across departments.

Career Path

This role is often filled by leaders already working in operations or project management, who then receive 3–6 months of targeted AI collaboration training. With experience, Orchestrators evolve into strategic advisors on workforce design and enterprise AI deployment.

The Prompt Engineer / AI Interaction Designer ($80K-120K annually)

Role: The "Communications Expert" Between Humans and AI

Every AI agent needs more than data and algorithms to succeed—it needs a human architect to define how it behaves, communicates, and integrates into the business. The **Agent Interaction Designer** crafts the instructions, guardrails, and interaction patterns that shape agent performance. Their work ensures that agents reflect the organization's brand, adhere to policies, and deliver reliable, high-quality outputs in every interaction.

Core Responsibilities:

- **Agent Persona Development:** Designing how agents "speak" and behave, particularly in customer-facing roles, to protect brand identity and trust.
- **Instruction Architecture:** Building the frameworks, prompts, and rules that guide agent reliability and consistency.
- **Quality Optimization:** Refining responses through continuous feedback loops and performance analysis.

- **Integration Design:** Embedding agents into business processes and technology ecosystems without friction.
- **Testing and Validation:** Running structured evaluations to confirm agent accuracy, compliance, and resilience across diverse scenarios.

Skills Profile:

Designers combine **technical writing expertise, user experience design, and an understanding of AI's strengths and limitations**. They must also excel at business communication, bridging the gap between leadership intent and agent execution.

Hire vs. Outsource Decision:

For many organizations, scale dictates the approach. Companies with fewer than 500 employees often **outsource this function initially** (typically **$5K–15K per month**) to accelerate adoption. As needs become clearer, they transition to **in-house hires** who can embed knowledge, adapt to strategy shifts, and scale long-term capability.

The AI Ethics & Compliance Officer ($110K-160K annually)

Role: The "Conscience and Shield" of Your AI Operations

AI agents can only deliver sustained business value if they operate inside trusted boundaries. The **AI Governance Lead** safeguards trust by ensuring that every deployment aligns with legal, ethical, and brand standards, while still driving a competitive advantage. This role is central to risk management, regulatory compliance, and building the confidence that both employees and external stakeholders need to fully embrace AI.

Core Responsibilities:

- **Regulatory Compliance:** Interpreting and applying industry-specific and regional regulations so every deployment meets evolving legal obligations.
- **Bias Detection and Mitigation:** Monitoring outputs for unfair or discriminatory patterns and establishing correction mechanisms.
- **Brand Protection:** Preserving organizational voice, tone, and values across all AI–human interactions.
- **Risk Assessment:** Identifying potential downsides of new use cases and designing mitigation strategies before problems arise.
- **Audit and Reporting:** Maintaining transparent documentation and reporting processes that satisfy internal governance needs and external oversight.

Skills Profile: Effective Governance Leads typically bring a legal or compliance background combined with a working knowledge of AI bias, fairness, and risk management. They must also demonstrate analytical strength and cross-functional influence to bridge technical, legal, and strategic domains.

Critical Importance:

Trust is the adoption bottleneck. Employees and customers will only embrace AI if they believe it is safe, fair, and aligned with the organization's values. Without this role, AI risks becoming sidelined—undermining investment and slowing competitive progress.

Hire vs. Outsource Decision Framework

Factor	Hire In-House	Outsource to Specialists
Budget Available	>$500K annually for AI initiatives	<$500K annually for AI initiatives
Timeline Pressure	6+ months acceptable for full deployment	Need measurable results in 2-3 months
Control Requirements	High control needed over processes/data	Comfortable with external management
Risk Tolerance	Low risk tolerance, need full oversight	Moderate risk acceptable for faster results
Strategic Importance	AI as core competitive advantage	AI for operational efficiency improvement
Internal Expertise	Have technical team capable of development	Limited internal AI/ML expertise

Most organizations succeed by starting with a hybrid model. They bring the AI Agent Orchestrator in-house to build operational fluency, while outsourcing Prompt Engineering and Ethics/Compliance expertise during the early stages. This approach provides them with immediate access to specialized skills, reduces upfront hiring risk, and enables leadership to refine long-term needs before committing to permanent roles.

4. Leading the Change: From Resistance to Adoption

The hardest part of agent adoption isn't technical - it's human. AI implementations succeed or fail based on leadership and effective change management, rather than the algorithms themselves.

The Three-Step Change Management Playbook

Step 1: Communicate the "Why" (Weeks 1-2) *Frame Enhancement, Not Replacement*

The most successful transformations begin not with technology, but with communication. Employees must hear a clear, compelling case for why AI agents represent an opportunity rather than a threat. As such, leaders must frame AI as an enhancement, not a replacement. Effective communication demonstrates to employees that agents eliminate repetitive work, allowing people to focus on higher-value activities.

Effective Messaging Framework

- **Position agents as productivity multipliers**: Emphasise how they reduce repetitive tasks and free employees for strategic work.
- **Use specific examples**: Show how agents enhance human skills rather than replace them.
- **Address fears openly**: Hold honest discussions about role evolution and the new opportunities it creates.
- **Provide competitive context**: Demonstrate how adoption strengthens market position and secures long-term relevance.

Communication Channels

- **Town halls with live Q&A** to establish transparency at scale.
- **Department-specific sessions** tailored to each team's concerns and opportunities.
- **One-to-one manager conversations** for personal reassurance and context.
- **Real-world role evolution stories**, showing employees that jobs evolve, not disappear.

Step 2: Create Evangelists (Weeks 3-8) *Identify and Empower Champions*

Adoption spreads more quickly through peer influence than through mandates. Research consistently shows that employees trust colleagues who share real stories of impact more than they trust leadership directives. Successful transformations identify natural champions—typically 15–20% of the workforce—and empower them as early adopters. These champions become storytellers, demonstrating how agents save hours, boost quality, and improve customer outcomes. Recognition and access to leadership amplify their influence.

Champion Selection Criteria:

- **Natural curiosity** about new technologies and processes

- **Influence within their peer groups** and credibility among colleagues
- **Process improvement mindset** with a history of successful change adoption
- **Strong communication skills** to explain benefits and address challenges

Champion Empowerment Program:

- **Advanced Training:** 40–60 hours of intensive AI collaboration practice
- **Early Access:** First opportunity to test new agent capabilities
- **Success Metrics:** Clear KPIs to measure and showcase value creation
- **Recognition Systems:** Public acknowledgment of contributions and results
- **Feedback Channels:** Direct lines to leadership for raising ideas or concerns

Success Story Documentation: Champions document and share specific examples of how agents have improved their work:

- Time savings
- Quality improvements
- Newly enabled capabilities
- Customer satisfaction gains
- ROI from new projects worked on

Step 3: Invest in Training (Weeks 6-12) *Build Organizational AI Collaboration Capabilities*

The most effective organizations treat AI collaboration as a core skill within their workforce. Training should scale across the organization, from foundational awareness for all employees to advanced customization for specialists and champions. Delivery methods matter: hands-on workshops, microlearning, peer mentoring, and targeted coaching build confidence and embed learning into daily routines. The outcome is not just awareness, but a workforce empowered to collaborate effectively and responsibly with agents.

Training Program Architecture:

Equipping employees to collaborate effectively with AI agents requires more than technical familiarization. It calls for a structured development pathway that scales from broad awareness to deep specialization. Leaders who architect training in this way create resilience, unlock measurable productivity, and build a culture where humans and AI work as partners rather than competitors.

Foundation Level (All Employees - 8 hours):

At this stage, every employee develops essential literacy in how AI agents function and their role within daily operations. The objective is not mastery, but confidence and trust.

- **Understanding AI agent capabilities and limitations**: demystifying what agents can and cannot do to reduce fear and misuse.
- **Basic collaboration principles and best practices**: establishing norms for human–AI interaction to ensure consistent work across teams.
- **Security and compliance requirements**: embedding responsible use from the outset to reduce organizational risk.
- **Escalation procedures and human override protocols**: ensuring people know when and how to intervene, safeguarding accountability.

Intermediate Level (Direct Agent Users - 20 hours):

For employees whose roles involve daily agent interaction, training deepens into operational excellence. This is where efficiency gains become visible.

- **Advanced collaboration techniques and optimization strategies**: refining prompts, workflows, and communication styles to maximise agent value.
- **Performance monitoring and quality assurance**: teaching teams to validate output, identify errors, and sustain trust in results.
- **Problem-solving and troubleshooting procedures**: preparing users to handle breakdowns without escalating unnecessarily.
- **Cross-functional coordination with agent-enhanced teams**: enabling smooth collaboration when agents are distributed across departments.

Advanced Level (Champions and Specialists - 40+ hours):

A small cohort evolves into in-house experts who both guide adoption and shape strategy. Their role is to amplify value across the organization.

- **Agent customisation and performance optimization**: tailoring agents to specific workflows and business needs.
- **Advanced integration techniques and workflow design**: embedding agents into enterprise systems for end-to-end efficiency.
- **Training and mentoring other team members**: creating a multiplier effect by building organizational capability.

- **Strategic planning for expanded agent deployment**: aligning technical capacity with business priorities to drive growth.

Training Delivery Methods:

Training employees to collaborate with AI agents is not a classroom exercise. It demands approaches that embed learning into daily work, accelerate adoption, and ensure that skills stick long after formal sessions end. The following methods combine practicality with impact, helping organizations translate training into measurable business value.

Hands-On Workshops. Employees learn best by doing. Live sessions built around real agent interaction replace abstract theory with direct experience. By experimenting in a safe environment, teams develop confidence and immediately see how AI can simplify their tasks.

Peer Mentoring. Champions and early adopters act as multipliers, guiding colleagues through everyday scenarios. This model not only teaches practical skills but also fosters trust in the technology, as employees learn from peers who share their own challenges.

Microlearning Modules. Short, focused lessons integrated into the flow of work allow busy professionals to upskill without disruption. Bite-sized modules reinforce key concepts over time, ensuring that knowledge compounds rather than fades after a single training day.

Performance Coaching. Individualised guidance helps employees refine their own use of AI agents. Coaching sessions address specific workflows, challenges, or goals, turning general training into targeted performance improvement.

Conclusion

Building an AI agent is only 20% of the challenge. The other 80% involves designing the organization around it—new roles, new skills, new culture, structured change management, and systematic training—where sustainable value emerges.

The companies that will dominate the next decade are those that invest as much in redesigning their teams, processes, and culture as they do in the technology itself.

This isn't an IT project. It's an executive leadership's mandate.

CHAPTER 4

Your Minimum Viable Toolchain & "Hello, World!" AI Agent

You've mapped the landscape and seen why agentic AI is a platform shift on par with mobile. You can now tell the difference between a reactive chatbot and a truly agentic system that plans, tools, and acts.

Next, we build your Minimum Viable Toolchain: a focused stack that small teams can master quickly, without the need for enterprise budgets. Then we put it to work by shipping a lean Python agent that tackles a real cost center for most organizations: intelligent email triage.

The aim is not to make you a programmer. It is to give you the technical literacy to choose the right tools, lead the build, and scale agent initiatives with confidence.

Our "Hello, World!" isn't a toy script that prints a line. It's a working Email Triage Agent—one that reads incoming customer emails, infers intent, and either routes them to the right team or drafts a smart reply. In other words: a first agent that delivers real value on day one.

Selecting the Right Toolchain for your Business

You face a choice: Code-First or Low-Code. Both can get your agent off the ground, but they set very different long-term trajectories.

Code-First is like laying down your own transport system. It is expensive at the start, but built exactly for your city and infinitely scalable. Low-Code is more like public transit. It is quick to board and easy to use, but you're always limited to the routes that someone else has chosen.

The Code-First Path: Maximum Control, Maximum Potential

The natural choice here is Python. Its syntax reads almost like plain English, which makes it the go-to language for AI. Simple to learn, powerful to scale—that's why it dominates agent development.

LangChain/LangGraph: Python Frameworks to Orchestrate Agentic Systems

LangChain is the toolkit for building AI workflows step by step. Think: pull in data, split it into chunks, summarize it, then use the summary to answer questions. It's modular: loaders bring in content, splitters divide text, chains manage flow, and memory maintains context for chat apps. You can even mix models inside the same workflow.

LangGraph takes this further. It's built for multi-agent, stateful systems where workflows aren't straight lines but evolving conversations. Instead of a single chain, you get a graph: nodes as actions, edges as transitions. That means loops, branching paths, and the ability to circle back when conditions change.

The killer feature? Shared state management. Every agent can access the same context and task list, making it perfect for dynamic systems like a task manager that adapts to new user requests on the fly.

- **LangChain** = chains. Great for clean, linear tasks like data retrieval → processing → output.
- **LangGraph** = graphs. Built for complex, adaptive interactions where context shifts midstream.

For our Email Triage Agent, LangChain provides a head start with ready-made components for email handling, API connections (Google AI, OpenAI, Anthropic), and built-in orchestration features such as error recovery and human escalation.

Vector Databases: Contextual Memory for Intelligent Decisions

Vector databases serve as sophisticated "memory palaces" for AI systems: storing and organizing information to enable AI to gain an understanding of context, relationships, and meaning rather than just exact word matches. This is possible because vector embeddings represent information in a way that captures meaning and relationships, enabling searches based on similarity rather than exact wording.

Vector databases are the memory palaces of AI. Instead of storing information like a filing cabinet, they organize knowledge so systems can recall meaning and relationships—not just keywords.

Here's how: when text enters an AI model, it's converted into vector embeddings—lists of numbers that capture semantic essence.

For example:

- ***"budget"*** might be [6.8, 1.9, 4.4, 2.2].
- ***"affordable"*** might be [6.6, 2.0, 4.7, 1.99].

Because these vectors sit close together in numerical space, the system knows they're related—even without exact word matches.

That's why a query like *"ways to save money on a family vacation"* can return a document titled *"affordable holiday destinations for parents with kids."* A traditional keyword search would miss it.

In short:

- **Traditional DBs** = filing cabinets. Retrieve only if the word matches.

- **Vector DBs** = expert librarians. Understand the meaning and find contextually relevant answers.

This capability turns AI from a keyword matcher into a reasoning partner.

This kind of logic is only practical with LLMs. In traditional programming, we would have to manually list every possible keyword or variation that someone might use, which would quickly become unfeasible or even impossible, as languages are so rich and diverse. LLMs generate embeddings that capture meaning, allowing the system to generalize and find relevant content without an exhaustive list of keywords.

Traditional databases, which depend on keyword-based searches, function like filing cabinets organized alphabetically. They retrieve documents if the search terms match the content. Vector databases are more like librarians who understand the meaning behind each document and can find relevant information based on context, even when the wording differs.

Low-Code Alternatives

N8n: Visual Workflow Builder with AI Integration

n8n is automation you can see. You build workflows on a canvas, dragging nodes like Lego bricks: one for Gmail, one for an AI model, one for Slack. Connect them with lines, and you've built a live system.

For an Email Triage Agent, the flow is simple:

1. **Trigger** → A Gmail node (OAuth-secured) fires whenever a new email arrives.
2. **Brain** → The content goes to an AI node (Gemini, OpenAI, or Anthropic) with a prompt to detect intent.
3. **Decision** → A Router node classifies the result ("Sales Inquiry," "Support Request," etc.).
4. **Actions** → Each branch triggers the right outcome. A sales inquiry, for example, creates a Salesforce lead and alerts the sales team in Slack.

Result: a no-code orchestration layer that turns incoming emails into instant, intelligent action.

With n8n, you can spin up this entire agent in an afternoon, without writing a single line of code. Operations teams don't have to wait on developers; they can design, adjust, and own their own AI-driven workflows. The result? Incredible operational agility and responsiveness at startup speed.

Airtable: The Flexible Backend

Airtable is often called a "spreadsheet on steroids." For our agent, it's both the control center and the dashboard.

1. Configuration Hub

Hard-coding rules into workflows is brittle. By storing them in Airtable, business teams can make changes instantly without requiring developers.

Example: Sales leads used to route to sales@company.com. You hire Alex. A manager edits one field in Airtable to reroute leads to alex@company.com. From that moment, every lead lands in Alex's inbox without touching n8n or code.

This cleanly separates logic (the workflow) from configuration (the rules).

2. Monitoring & Analytics Layer

Airtable also doubles as a visibility platform. Every processed email is logged, including the sender, subject, AI-detected intent, and the action taken. With Airtable views, you can:

- Track volumes (sales vs. support inquiries)
- Spot customer trends
- Flag misclassifications for review

The result: not just automation, but real-time business intelligence.

Often described as a "spreadsheet on steroids," Airtable is a user-friendly relational database. For our agent, it plays two crucial roles:

1. The Configuration Hub

Where should the agent's rules live? In a code-first setup, routing logic (e.g., "If intent = Billing Question, then forward to finance@") would be hard-coded. That's inflexible and brittle. By storing them in Airtable, business teams can make changes instantly without requiring developers.

Our n8n workflow can query Airtable to decide the correct action based on the AI's classification. This means that business users can update a record in Airtable to change the workflow without needing to touch n8n or code. If your sales process changes, a manager can simply edit a field in Airtable to reroute leads.

For example, suppose your sales inquiry emails currently go to sales@company.com, but you've just hired a new rep who should handle all inbound leads. Instead of editing the n8n workflow, a manager can simply update the "Forward To" field in Airtable from sales@company.com to alex@company.com. From that moment on, every new lead is automatically routed to Alex—no developer needed.

This cleanly separates logic (the n8n workflow) from configuration (the rules).

2. The Monitoring and Analytics Layer

Airtable also doubles as a visibility platform. Every processed email is logged, including the sender, subject, AI-detected intent, and the action taken. With Airtable views, you can:

- Track volumes (sales vs. support inquiries)
- Spot customer trends
- Flag misclassifications for review

The result: not just automation, but real-time business intelligence. A production system must not be a black box. By logging every processed email into Airtable, we can create a lightweight monitoring platform. Each record can capture the sender, subject, AI-classified intent, and action taken. This gives instant visibility into how the agent works.

Airtable's views and dashboards track volumes (e.g., sales vs. support inquiries), spot patterns in customer communication, and even review cases where the classification may need correction. This transforms the workflow from a simple automation into a source of actionable business intelligence.

Comparative Framework: Making the Strategic Choice

Decision Factor	**Code-First (Python/LangChain)**	**Low-Code (N8n/Airtable)**
Initial Setup Time	2-4 weeks with technical team	2-4 days with business users
Monthly Operating Costs	$70-2,000+ (scales with volume)	$30-2,000+ (scales with usage)
Customization Ceiling	Unlimited - build anything	Limited by platform capabilities
Skills Required	Python developers, DevOps expertise	Business analysts, process knowledge
Scalability	Handles millions of emails efficiently	Platform limits may require upgrades
Integration Flexibility	Connect to any system via APIs	Limited to supported connectors
Maintenance Overhead	Requires technical team for updates	Platform handles infrastructure
Vendor Lock-in Risk	Own your code and data	Dependent on platform continuity

Code-First Adoption is Appropriate When:

- Developing AI-first products requiring sophisticated reasoning
- Managing high transaction volumes with cost optimization goals
- Integrating proprietary models or custom AI logic
- Operating in regulated industries with defined compliance needs
- Supported by technically capable teams with DevOps maturity
- Seeking to differentiate competitively through AI capability

Low-Code Adoption is Appropriate When:

- Requiring rapid deployment of business process automation
- Engaging non-technical teams or working with limited development resources
- Connecting standard SaaS platforms and enterprise applications
- Operating under constrained budgets or resources
- Prioritizing reliability and vendor support over customization
- Piloting AI concepts before committing significant investment

In practice, most organizations typically begin with low-code implementations to generate quick wins and validate business value. Over time, high-volume or specialized workflows have migrated to code-first solutions to unlock efficiency and gain a competitive advantage.

This staged approach not only accelerates adoption but also develops organizational literacy, enabling more informed decisions about where custom development yields the highest return on investment.

This approach also helps prove business value quickly through low-code prototypes. It also makes it easier to identify scaling bottlenecks before making major technical investments. At the same time, it supports building internal AI literacy across both business and technical teams. Ultimately, it enables informed decisions about where custom development provides the best return on investment.

Building the Agent

The Business Problem: Death by a Thousand Emails

Every company has them: **support@, sales@, info@.** They serve as the digital front doors for customers, partners, and prospects.

For a small business, these inboxes are manageable. For a growing enterprise, they become productivity black holes.

Consider this: the average professional spends 28% of the day in email. For a non-sales or support role, that's a distraction. For support staff, much of that time is wasted on manual triage—reading, interpreting, and forwarding messages.

A five-person team managing a shared inbox can burn through 2,000+ hours a year and over $100,000 in pay just sorting mail. That's time that could be spent solving problems, closing deals, or serving customers.

Our Solution: How the Agent "Thinks" About Email Intent

Our agent's code will mimic the decision-making process of professionals. Its logic follows the classic Perceive-Think-Act loop.

1. **Perceive:** The agent ingests the raw text of a new email.
2. **Think:** A classification function applies a structured prompt to the language model. The model is constrained to return one of four intents: *Sales Inquiry, Technical Support, Billing Question,* or *General Inquiry.* The system validates the result and defaults to *General Inquiry* when responses fall outside these categories, providing consistency and control.
3. **Act:** The route_email function maps each intent to action. Sales go into the CRM. Billing goes to Finance. Support routes to the right queue.

This simple loop can turn a chaotic inbox into an intelligent, automated workflow.

Looking Under the Hood: Our Functional Agent

```
# Email Classification System
import os
from typing import Dict, Optional
from langchain_google_genai import ChatGoogleGenerativeAI
from langchain_core.prompts import ChatPromptTemplate
from langchain_core.output_parsers import StrOutputParser

# Load environment variables from .env file
from dotenv import load_dotenv
load_dotenv()  # This loads the .env file automatically

class EmailClassifier:
    """Email classification system with improved error handling and
flexibility."""

    VALID_INTENTS = ["Sales Inquiry", "Technical Support", "Billing Question",
"General Inquiry"]

    def __init__(self, model_name: str = "gemini-1.5-flash-latest"):
        """Initialize the classifier with API key validation."""
        if "GOOGLE_API_KEY" not in os.environ:
            raise ValueError(
                "Google API key not found. Please create a .env file with:\n"
                "GOOGLE_API_KEY=your-api-key-here"
            )

        self.llm = ChatGoogleGenerativeAI(api_key=os.environ["GOOGLE_API_KEY"],
model=model_name)
        self.classifier_chain = self._build_classifier_chain()

    def _build_classifier_chain(self):
        """Build the classification chain with improved prompt."""
        prompt = ChatPromptTemplate.from_template(
            """
            Analyze the following email content and classify its primary intent.

            Return EXACTLY one of these classifications (case-sensitive):
            - Sales Inquiry
            - Technical Support
            - Billing Question
            - General Inquiry

            Guidelines:
            - Sales Inquiry: Questions about pricing, products, purchases, demos
            - Technical Support: Problems, bugs, how-to questions,
troubleshooting
            - Billing Question: Payment issues, invoices, charges, account
billing
            - General Inquiry: Company info, general questions, feedback

            Email Content:
            {email_text}

            Classification:"""
        )
        return prompt | self.llm | StrOutputParser()

    def classify_email(self, email_content: str) -> Optional[str]:
        """Classify email intent with error handling."""
        try:
            intent = self.classifier_chain.invoke({"email_text": email_content})
            # Clean and validate the response
            intent = intent.strip()

            # Handle common variations
            if intent in self.VALID_INTENTS:
                return intent
```

```
            # Try to match with case-insensitive comparison
            for valid_intent in self.VALID_INTENTS:
                if intent.lower() == valid_intent.lower():
                    return valid_intent

            print(f"Warning: Unexpected classification '{intent}', defaulting to
General Inquiry")
            return "General Inquiry"

        except Exception as e:
            print(f"Error classifying email: {e}")
            return None

    def route_email(self, email_content: str) -> Dict[str, str]:
        """Route email and return action details."""
        intent = self.classify_email(email_content)

        if intent is None:
            return {"intent": None, "action": "Error processing email",
"status": "failed"}

        # Define routing actions
        actions = {
            "Sales Inquiry": "Routing to Sales CRM",
            "Technical Support": "Creating support ticket",
            "Billing Question": "Forwarding to Finance department",
            "General Inquiry": "Drafting a general response"
        }

        action = actions.get(intent, "Drafting a general response")

        result = {
            "intent": intent,
            "action": action,
            "status": "success"
        }

        print(f"Intent: {intent}")
        print(f"ACTION: {action}")

        return result
    # Usage example with improved error handling
    def main():
        """Test the improved email classifier."""
        try:
            classifier = EmailClassifier()

            # Test cases
            test_emails = [
                "Hello, I was wondering how much your enterprise plan costs.
    Thanks!",
                "I'm having trouble logging into my account. Can you help?",
                "I was charged twice this month. Please check my billing.",
                "What are your office hours and location?",
                "The software keeps crashing when I try to export data.",
            ]

            for i, email in enumerate(test_emails, 1):
                print(f"\n=== Test Email {i} ===")
                print(f"Email: {email}")
                result = classifier.route_email(email)
                print(f"Result: {result}")

        except Exception as e:
            print(f"Setup error: {e}")

    if __name__ == "__main__":
        main()
```

Caveats: From "Hello World" to Production

What we've built is a proof of concept. It is powerful, but not yet enterprise-grade. To reach production, your team would layer on several essentials:

- **Execution capability.** At present, the agent outputs intended actions. A production-grade agent would integrate with business applications through secure APIs to execute tasks—such as creating Zendesk tickets, updating Salesforce records, or interfacing with financial systems.
- **Error management.** Robust error handling would be necessary to address external system downtime or API failures, ensuring service continuity.
- **Monitoring and reporting.** Enterprise systems require transparency. Every action would be logged and surfaced in a performance dashboard, capturing metrics such as email volume, classification accuracy, and processing time.
- **Security and compliance.** Integration into the corporate IT environment would involve authenticated access to email, secure storage of API keys and credentials, and adherence to organizational data governance and security standards.

These measures transform the prototype from a working demonstration into a production-ready enterprise capability. The difference is not intelligence; it's integration, resilience, and trust.

Conclusion

You've seen the journey: from a costly inbox bottleneck to a working agent, powered by real code. Along the way, you've learned the essentials, i.e., why toolchain choices matter, how prompts shape outcomes, and how an agent can perceive, think, and act.

But let's be clear: this agent solves one problem, and one problem only. It classifies and routes emails. Valuable, yes, but only the first rung of the ladder.

What happens when processes demand more? Imagine an agent that not only classifies but also searches your knowledge base, summarizes key points, and drafts a personalized reply, ready to be sent.

That's where we go next: expanding from a single-task agent to a multi-step workflow using LangChain.

References:

- https://www.mckinsey.com/capabilities/mckinsey-digital/our-insights/superagency-in-the-workplace-empowering-people-to-unlock-ais-full-potential-at-work

CHAPTER 5

From Single Tasks to Workflows

Automation has always promised efficiency with fewer clicks, faster delegations, and lower costs. But efficiency alone isn't enough when customer relationships are at stake. The email classification agent we built in Chapter 4 performs admirably within its narrow scope. It reads an incoming message, determines its intent, and announces its routing decision. For many organizations, this level of automation represents a significant productivity gain. But classification alone is inadequate: real customer issues rarely stay confined to neat categories, and their scope often extends beyond a single label.

Consider this customer email:

> *"Hi, I've been trying to update my payment method for the past week, but your billing portal keeps giving me an error. My subscription expires tomorrow, and I really can't afford any downtime with the client presentation I have on Friday. Can someone please help me resolve this urgently?"*

Our Chapter 4 agent might confidently classify this as a "Billing Question" and route it to the finance department. Technically correct, but strategically inadequate. This is not a billing inquiry. It is an at-risk customer expressing urgency regarding potential service disruption, with a clear business-critical deadline. As this stands, the finance team might resolve the payment issue within their standard two-day timeframe. Still, by then, the customer's subscription will have lapsed, their client presentation will have failed, and what began as a simple update will have become a cancellation and a potentially damaging business review.

The fundamental limitation of single-task agents is that they optimize for local efficiency while missing global context. Our first agent successfully categorized the email, but failed to achieve the broader business objective of ensuring customer success.

This gap between task completion and business outcome is the difference between automation and intelligence. Automation executes predefined processes. Intelligence adapts the process to achieve the desired business outcome.

This chapter shows how to transform our simple agent from an email classifier into a strategist. Instead of making a single decision and stopping, our enhanced agent will engage in multi-step reasoning to gather context, assess urgency, and execute a coordinated workflow designed to maximize customer retention.

Thinking in Steps

Our Chapter 4 agent embodied what we might call "oracle thinking". It received a question, consulted its knowledge, and delivered a final answer. This pattern works well for simple classification tasks but breaks down when an optimal response requires gathering additional information or when the initial assessment reveals unexpected complexity.

The Problem with Single Decisions

Consider how our billing question example would flow through our existing agent:

Input: "I've been trying to update my payment method..."

Classification: "Billing Question"

Action: "Forwarding to Finance department"

Status: Complete

The agent has missed a critical context that would change the appropriate response. It doesn't know that this is a long-term customer, that their subscription is expiring imminently, or that they have an urgent business need. A human triaging this same email would naturally ask: "Who is this customer? What's their account status? How urgent is this really?"

This is where the **ReAct pattern** comes in handy to transform agent behavior from.

The Investigation Loop

As we discussed in Chapter 2, ReAct reflects the approach of skilled professionals to complex problems. Rather than making immediate decisions based on limited information, the agent engages in a deliberate cycle of analysis, action, and learning.

This is how an enhanced agent might handle the same billing email using ReAct:

Cycle 1:

- **Reason**: "This appears to be a billing issue, but the mention of 'urgent' and 'client presentation' suggests higher stakes. I should gather customer context before routing."
- **Act**: Query CRM for customer account details
- **Observe**: The customer is on the Enterprise plan, a 3-year subscriber, with renewal due in 24 hours, valued at $50K annually.

Cycle 2:

- **Reason**: "High-value customer with imminent renewal risk. The 'client presentation Friday' creates time pressure. This needs escalated handling, not standard billing queue."
- **Act**: Check current support queue volumes and available senior agents.
- **Observe**: Senior billing specialist available, standard queue has a 2-day backlog.

Cycle 3:

- **Reason**: "Direct assignment to senior specialist bypasses queue delay. The customer needs proactive communication about status and timeline."
- **Act**: Assign to a senior specialist with a priority flag and auto-generate an acknowledgment of an email with the expected resolution time.
- **Observe**: Assignment confirmed, customer notified with 4-hour resolution commitment.

Each **Observe** phase provides new information that influences the next **Reason** phase. The agent builds understanding progressively rather than making assumptions based on initial appearances.

Code Implementation: Adding ReAct to Our Agent

Here's how we extend our EmailClassifier to support ReAct reasoning:

```
class TriageAgent(EmailClassifier):
    def __init__(self):
        super().__init__()
        self.max_reasoning_steps = 5
        self.tools = {
            'crm_lookup': self._query_customer_data,
            'check_queue': self._check_support_queue,
            'assign_ticket': self._create_assignment
        }

    def enhanced_triage(self, email_content, customer_email):
        """ReAct loop for intelligent email triage"""
        context = {"email": email_content, "customer": customer_email}

        for step in range(self.max_reasoning_steps):
            # REASON: Analyze current context and decide next action
            reasoning = self._reason_about_context(context)

            if reasoning['action'] == 'COMPLETE':
                return reasoning['final_decision']

            # ACT: Execute the determined action
            tool_name = reasoning['tool_to_use']
            action_result = self.tools[tool_name](reasoning['parameters'])

            # OBSERVE: Update context with new information
            context.update({f'step_{step}_result': action_result})

        # Fallback if max steps reached
        return self._make_final_decision(context)
```

NB: The code snippets presented throughout this chapter are designed for clarity and illustrative purposes. They have been intentionally streamlined to highlight the core strategic logic and business rules, free from the necessary complexity of a production-ready system.

For those who wish to explore the full Python script for the Enhanced Triage Agent, it will be available in the Appendix as well as in an interactive Google Colab linked at the end of this chapter.

Loop Termination and Goal Achievement

Critical to ReAct implementation is knowing when to stop reasoning and take final action. Our agent uses several termination conditions:

1. **Sufficient Information**: When confidence in the routing decision exceeds the threshold.
2. **Diminishing Returns**: When additional queries aren't yielding useful new data.
3. **Time Constraints**: When response time requirements demand immediate action.
4. **Max Steps**: Preventing infinite loops with reasonable step limits.

Error Handling in Reasoning Loops

Unlike single-step processes, ReAct loops must handle failures gracefully:

```
def _safe_tool_execution(self, tool_name, parameters):
    """Execute tool with fallback handling"""
    try:
        return self.tools[tool_name](parameters)
    except APIError:
        return {"error": "service_unavailable", "fallback":
"use_default_routing"}
    except TimeoutError:
        return {"error": "timeout", "fallback": "escalate_to_human"}
```

When a CRM lookup fails, the agent notes the limitation and adjusts its reasoning accordingly, rather than crashing. It can, for instance, default to conservative escalation rather than standard routing.

Building the Enhanced Triage Agent

The ReAct pattern provides the cognitive framework, but building a production-ready triage agent requires translating that reasoning capability into concrete business actions. This means evolving our architecture from a single LLM call to a sophisticated workflow engine that can gather intelligence, assess context, and orchestrate responses across multiple business systems.

Architecture Evolution: From Static to Dynamic

Our Chapter 4 agent followed a rigid pattern: classify intent, announce the routing decision, and terminate the process. The enhanced triage agent operates more like a detective building a case:

1. **Initial Assessment**: Quick classification to understand the general category.
2. **Context Gathering**: Strategic queries to build situational awareness.
3. **Priority Evaluation**: Assessment of urgency, customer value, and business impact.
4. **Response Orchestration**: Coordinated actions across appropriate systems.
5. **Confirmation and Follow-up**: Verification that handoffs succeeded and next steps are clear.

New Capabilities: The Intelligence Layer

Customer Context Lookup

Instead of treating every email as isolated, our agent now queries customer relationship systems to understand account history, subscription status, and past interaction patterns.

```
def _gather_customer_context(self, customer_email):
    """Build comprehensive customer profile"""
    context = {}

    # Account fundamentals
    account_data = self.crm_client.get_customer(customer_email)
    context['tier'] = account_data.get('subscription_level', 'basic')
    context['tenure'] = account_data.get('months_active', 0)
    context['ltv'] = account_data.get('lifetime_value', 0)

    # Recent interaction history
    recent_tickets = self.support_client.get_recent_tickets(customer_email,
days=30)
    context['recent_issues'] = len(recent_tickets)
    context['escalation_history'] = any(ticket.priority == 'high' for ticket
in recent_tickets)

    # Account health indicators
    context['payment_current'] = account_data.get('billing_status') ==
'current'
    context['renewal_date'] = account_data.get('next_renewal')

    return context
Urgency Assessment Through Multi-Factor Analysis Rather than relying on
keywords like "urgent," the agent evaluates urgency through business logic:
def _calculate_urgency_score(self, email_content, customer_context):
    """Multi-dimensional urgency assessment"""
    score = 0
    factors = []

    # Time-based urgency indicators
    if 'today' in email_content.lower() or 'asap' in email_content.lower():
        score += 3
        factors.append('explicit_time_pressure')

    # Customer value weighting
    if customer_context['tier'] == 'enterprise':
        score += 2
        factors.append('high_value_customer')

    # Business continuity risk
    service_keywords = ['down', 'outage', 'not working', 'broken']
    if any(keyword in email_content.lower() for keyword in
service_keywords):
        score += 4
        factors.append('service_disruption')

    # Renewal risk assessment
    days_to_renewal =
self._days_until_renewal(customer_context['renewal_date'])
    if days_to_renewal <= 7:
        score += 2
        factors.append('renewal_risk')

    return {
        'urgency_score': score,
        'contributing_factors': factors,
        'priority_level': 'high' if score >= 6 else 'medium' if score >= 3
else 'low'
    }
```

Dynamic Routing Based on Combined Intelligence

With rich context and urgency assessment, routing decisions become sophisticated business logic:

```
def _determine_routing_strategy(self, classification, urgency_data,
customer_context):
    """Intelligent routing based on complete context"""

    # High-urgency enterprise customers get direct specialist assignment
    if urgency_data['priority_level'] == 'high' and customer_context['tier']
== 'enterprise':
        return {
            'method': 'direct_assignment',
            'target': self._find_senior_specialist(classification),
            'sla_hours': 2,
            'escalation_path': 'customer_success_manager'
        }

    # Renewal-risk customers need retention-focused handling
    if 'renewal_risk' in urgency_data['contributing_factors']:
        return {
            'method': 'retention_workflow',
            'target': 'customer_success_team',
            'sla_hours': 4,
            'auto_actions': ['flag_for_retention_review',
'schedule_check_in_call']
        }

    # Standard routing with context-aware prioritization
    return {
        'method': 'queue_assignment',
        'target': self._get_appropriate_queue(classification),
        'priority': urgency_data['priority_level'],
        'sla_hours': self._calculate_sla(customer_context['tier'],
urgency_data['priority_level'])
    }
```

Action Verification and Follow-up

Unlike fire-and-forget automation, the enhanced agent confirms successful handoffs and establishes clear next steps:

```
def _execute_routing_with_confirmation(self, routing_strategy, email_data,
context):
    """Execute routing with verification and follow-up"""

    # Create the ticket/assignment
    ticket_id = self._create_ticket(email_data, routing_strategy, context)

    # Verify successful creation
    if not self._verify_ticket_creation(ticket_id):
        return self._handle_creation_failure(email_data, routing_strategy)

    # Send customer acknowledgment
    acknowledgment = self._generate_customer_response(
        routing_strategy['sla_hours'],
        context['customer_tier']
    )
    self._send_acknowledgment_email(email_data['sender'], acknowledgment)

    # Set up follow-up triggers
    if routing_strategy.get('auto_actions'):
        self._schedule_follow_up_actions(ticket_id,
routing_strategy['auto_actions'])

    return {
        'status': 'success',
        'ticket_id': ticket_id,
        'estimated_resolution': routing_strategy['sla_hours'],
        'next_review': self._calculate_follow_up_time(routing_strategy)
    }
```

State Management Across Workflow Steps

As the agent progresses through its ReAct loop, it maintains a comprehensive state about its reasoning process, decisions made, and actions taken:

```
class TriageState:
    def __init__(self, email_data):
        self.email_data = email_data
        self.reasoning_history = []
        self.customer_context = {}
        self.urgency_assessment = {}
        self.routing_decision = {}
        self.actions_taken = []
        self.completion_status = 'in_progress'

    def add_reasoning_step(self, step_type, reasoning, action_taken,
result):
        """Track each step of the ReAct process"""
        self.reasoning_history.append({
            'step': len(self.reasoning_history) + 1,
            'type': step_type,
            'reasoning': reasoning,
            'action': action_taken,
            'result': result,
            'timestamp': datetime.utcnow()
        })
Error Handling and Graceful Degradation Production agents must handle system
failures without breaking the customer experience:
def _safe_context_gathering(self, customer_email):
    """Gather context with fallback for system unavailability"""
    context = {'source': 'minimal_fallback'}

    try:
        # Attempt full CRM lookup
        context.update(self._gather_customer_context(customer_email))
        context['source'] = 'full_crm_data'
    except CRMUnavailableError:
        # Use cached data if available
        cached_data = self._get_cached_customer_data(customer_email)
        if cached_data:
            context.update(cached_data)
            context['source'] = 'cached_data'
            context['data_freshness'] = 'stale'

    # Always have basic email domain analysis as final fallback
    context['domain_type'] = self._analyze_email_domain(customer_email)

    return context
```

When the CRM system is down, the agent doesn't fail; it adapts its reasoning to work with whatever information is available, potentially routing more conservatively but still providing intelligent triage.

The Transformation in Action

Let's trace our problematic billing email through the complete enhanced system:

Step 1: Initial classification confirms "billing issue" but triggers context gathering.

Step 2: CRM lookup reveals an enterprise customer with $50K ARR, with a renewal in 24 hours.

Step 3: Urgency assessment finds a high score due to time pressure + renewal risk, + customer value.

Step 4: Routing logic selects direct assignment to the senior billing specialist.

Step 5: Customer receives immediate acknowledgment with a 4-hour resolution commitment.

Step 6: Automatic follow-up scheduled for review by the retention team.

The same email input now generates a more effective business outcome.

This enhanced triage agent goes from task automation to business intelligence. Rather than simply categorizing and forwarding, it gathers intelligence, makes strategic assessments, and orchestrates coordinated responses designed to optimize business outcomes rather than just operational efficiency.

Tool Chaining for Complex Processes

The power of our enhanced triage agent lies not just in its reasoning capabilities but in its ability to orchestrate actions across multiple business systems. This requires moving beyond single API calls to sophisticated tool chaining—sequences of system interactions where each action provides context for the next decision.

The Tool Integration Challenge

Traditional automation connects Point A to Point B: an email arrives, and the system forwards it to the department. Agentic workflows create dynamic pathways that adapt based on the information they discover. Our agent might query the CRM, check inventory levels, verify payment status, schedule calendar appointments, and send personalized communications, all within a single customer interaction.

This orchestration requires careful handling of dependencies, authentication across systems, and graceful degradation when services are unavailable.

Sequential Tool Use: Building Context Progressively

Consider how our enhanced agent handles a complex technical support email from an enterprise customer reporting system downtime:

```
def _handle_technical_issue_workflow(self, email_data, customer_context):
    """Multi-step workflow for technical issue resolution"""
    s
    # Step 1: Check system status dashboard
    system_status = self.monitoring_client.get_current_status()

    # Step 2: If widespread issue, route to incident response
    if system_status.get('widespread_outage'):
        return self._escalate_to_incident_team(email_data, system_status)

    # Step 3: Check customer's specific environment
    customer_health = self.infrastructure_client.check_customer_environment(
        customer_context['account_id']
    )

    # Step 4: Query knowledge base for similar issues
    similar_issues = self.knowledge_client.search_solutions({
        'customer_tier': customer_context['tier'],
        'symptoms': self._extract_symptoms(email_data['content']),
        'environment': customer_health['platform_version']
    })

    # Step 5: Route based on combined intelligence
    if similar_issues and customer_health['status'] == 'healthy':
        return self._create_ticket_with_suggested_solutions(similar_issues)
    else:
        return self._escalate_to_senior_engineer(customer_health,
customer_context)
```

Each tool call informs the next decision. System status determines whether this is an individual or systemic issue. Customer environment health affects solution recommendations. Knowledge base results influence routing decisions.

Practical Implementation Considerations

API Authentication and Rate Limiting

Production tool chaining requires robust connection management:

```
class ToolChainOrchestrator:
    def __init__(self):
        self.connection_pool = {}
        self.rate_limiters = {}

    def _execute_tool_safely(self, tool_name, parameters):
        """Execute tool with rate limiting and retry logic"""
        rate_limiter = self.rate_limiters.get(tool_name)
        if rate_limiter and not rate_limiter.can_proceed():
            return {'status': 'rate_limited', 'retry_after':
rate_limiter.reset_time}

        try:
            connection = self._get_connection(tool_name)
            result = connection.execute(parameters)
            self._update_rate_limiter(tool_name)
            return {'status': 'success', 'data': result}
        except AuthenticationError:
            self._refresh_authentication(tool_name)
            return {'status': 'auth_retry_needed'}
        except APITimeoutError:
            return {'status': 'timeout', 'fallback_action':
'use_cached_data'}
```

Data Validation Between Systems

When chaining tools, data from one system becomes input to the next. Validation prevents cascade failures:

```
def _validate_customer_data(self, crm_data):
    """Ensure CRM data is suitable for downstream tools"""
    required_fields = ['account_id', 'tier', 'status']

    for field in required_fields:
        if field not in crm_data or crm_data[field] is None:
            raise DataValidationError(f"Missing required field: {field}")

    # Sanitize for downstream APIs
    return {
        'account_id': str(crm_data['account_id']),
        'tier': crm_data['tier'].lower().strip(),
        'status': crm_data['status']
    }
```

Performance Optimization and Parallelization

Some tool calls can be executed simultaneously to reduce latency:

```
import asyncio

async def _gather_parallel_context(self, customer_email):
    """Execute independent queries simultaneously"""

    # These operations don't depend on each other
    tasks = [
        self._async_crm_lookup(customer_email),
        self._async_support_history(customer_email),
        self._async_billing_status(customer_email)
    ]

    results = await asyncio.gather(*tasks, return_exceptions=True)

    # Combine results, handling any failures gracefully
    context = {}
    for i, result in enumerate(results):
        if isinstance(result, Exception):
            context[f'source_{i}_error'] = str(result)
        else:
            context.update(result)

    return context
```

Error Recovery and Rollback Procedures

When tool chains fail partway through, the agent needs recovery strategies:

```
def _handle_workflow_failure(self, workflow_state, failed_step):
    """Recover from mid-workflow failures"""

    # Log the failure for analysis
    self.logger.error(f"Workflow failed at step {failed_step}",
                      extra={'workflow_state': workflow_state})

    # Determine if partial completion is acceptable
    if workflow_state.get('ticket_created'):
        # We have a ticket, just need to update priority manually
        return self._fallback_to_manual_prioritization(workflow_state)

    # If no progress made, fall back to simple routing
    return self._execute_simple_classification_fallback(
        workflow_state['original_email']
    )
```

The Intelligence Multiplier Effect

What makes ReAct powerful for business applications is that each reasoning step can dramatically change the outcome. A simple billing question becomes an urgent retention issue. A routine technical support request reveals a systematic product problem affecting multiple customers. A general inquiry from a new email address turns out to be from a major prospect evaluating your company.

This adaptive intelligence is what separates truly useful AI systems from mere automation. The agent determines the appropriate workflow based on the specific context it encounters rather than merely executing predefined workflows.

The Economics of Intelligence

Training Time Reduction

New staff can be productive almost immediately with agent-assisted triage support rather than requiring 2-3 weeks to learn customer context, system relationships, and escalation procedures. The agent serves as an expert system that encodes institutional knowledge and expertise.

Customer Satisfaction Improvements

Customer satisfaction scores can increase by 10% after AI-assisted email triage reduces response times and misrouting. High-value customers particularly notice the difference when their inquiries receive appropriate prioritization automatically.

Scalability Without Linear Cost Increase

An agent handles volume increases without proportional staffing increases. A 50% growth in email volume requires only infrastructure scaling rather than hiring additional triage staff, fundamentally changing the economics of customer support operations.

The Strategic Intelligence Layer

Beyond operational improvements, the enhanced triage agent generates valuable business intelligence:

1. **Pattern Recognition**: Identification of recurring issues that suggest product improvements or documentation gaps.
2. **Customer Health Monitoring**: Early warning signals for at-risk accounts based on inquiry patterns and urgency trends.

Resource Optimization: Data-driven insights into peak volumes, staffing needs, and skill requirements.

3. **Competitive Intelligence**: Analysis of inquiry themes that reveal market pressures or competitive dynamics.

Compound Value Creation

The agent's value compounds in three ways:

1. **Learning Acceleration**: Each processed email improves the knowledge base and routing algorithms.
2. **Network Effects**: Better routing leads to faster resolution, which improves customer satisfaction and reduces future inquiry volume.
3. **Capability Expansion**: The infrastructure for intelligent triage becomes the foundation for automating other complex business processes.

A company implementing intelligent triage in Q1 often expands to automated lead qualification in Q2, intelligent document routing in Q3, and comprehensive customer journey automation by year-end. The initial investment in agentic infrastructure pays dividends across multiple business functions.

Conclusion: The Foundation for Intelligence

We began this chapter with a simple classifier and ended with a sophisticated workflow orchestrator that gathers intelligence, makes strategic assessments, and coordinates multi-system responses.

From a technical perspective, we've demonstrated how the ReAct pattern transforms reactive systems into proactive problem-solvers. By implementing Reason-Act-Observe loops, our agent moves beyond single-point decisions to progressive intelligence building. Each workflow execution generates data that improves future performance, creating a compounding advantage that static automation cannot match.

The foundation is built. The patterns are proven. Your organization can now transform any complex, high-volume business process from manual coordination to intelligent automation.

References:

- Case Study: Elevating Customer Interactions with AI and Automation
- Complete Enhanced Triage Agent in Google Colab

Chapter 6

Giving Your Agent Memory (The Knowledge Agent)

As your most experienced engineers retire, they take irreplaceable knowledge and expertise with them. Your workflow agents could coordinate tasks brilliantly, but they operate in a knowledge vacuum, unable to tap into the institutional wisdom that separates efficient task processing from intelligent problem-solving.

The workflow agent we built in Chapter 5 is an intelligent coordinator, but it operates with a limited memory. It can assess the urgency of a new request, but it cannot access the decades of accumulated expertise trapped within your organization's documents, support cases, and engineering notes.

Consider a high-value customer asking a complex question that references a past conversation with a business. Our Chapter 5 agent was able to correctly identify it as a high-priority ticket and route it to an expert. However, it couldn't provide the *substantive guidance* needed to actually solve the customer's unique problem. This gap between workflow intelligence and institutional wisdom is what distinguishes task processors from true problem solvers.

This issue extends far beyond a minor concern. It represents a crisis in how knowledge is accessed. Research shows the average knowledge worker spends 2.5 hours daily simply searching for information. While some searching is unavoidable, most of those 2.5 hours represent wasted effort. For an organization with 1,000 employees, that could mean millions of dollars in lost productivity every year. Critical insights are scattered across wikis, emails, and Slack, forcing teams to waste time and money just to find what they need.

RAG bridges this gap by providing agents with access to organizational memory. Like a skilled consultant with perfect recall, a RAG-enabled agent is able to consult your company's entire knowledge base and then provide informed, contextually relevant answers. This transformation converts a workflow agent into a knowledge agent: a system that provides actionable guidance based on your organization's collective intelligence.

How Agents Remember

Our goal is to give our agent an institutional memory, and as we know from earlier chapters, Retrieval-Augmented Generation (RAG) is the key. By connecting our agent to a vector database of company documents, we allow it to perform intelligent, semantic searches that understand context and keywords.

While the vector databases that power RAG are excellent at understanding semantic meaning (e.g., connecting "customer churn" to "retention strategies"), a purely semantic approach can fall short in a business context. It can sometimes miss critical keywords, specific product names, or financial acronyms.

Microsoft's Azure AI Search combines two different methods (vector + keyword) of retrieving information, and this hybrid approach *often outperforms* pure vector or keyword methods. In independent evaluations, hybrid models have achieved relative gains of ~20% over pure deep retrieval methods in cross-domain settings.

This is why leading enterprise implementations of knowledge agents now use a Hybrid Search approach. The practical impact becomes clear in enterprise scenarios. A query for "Q3 EBITDA projections" requires both semantic understanding (financial forecasting concepts) and keyword precision (Q3, EBITDA). Hybrid search ensures that both dimensions are captured, delivering more accurate and comprehensive results.

Building Your Knowledge Agent

Transforming the workflow agent from Chapter 5 into a knowledge-enabled system requires careful attention to how organizational information is prepared, stored, and retrieved. Our technical implementation builds on familiar patterns while adding the memory layer that enables institutional intelligence.

Document Preparation: Making Knowledge Accessible

The effectiveness of our knowledge agent rises or falls based on how well information is prepared for retrieval. Two levers dominate outcomes: how we chunk content and how we enrich it with metadata.

How information is broken down and labeled makes a big difference in how well an AI system retrieves answers. Break text into pieces that are too small, and the system may miss the bigger picture. Make them too large, and it may overlook key details. The right balance depends on your business context, so it's essential to start with a sensible default and adjust it based on your specific needs. Multi-dataset analyses show a clear trade-off: smaller chunks (≈ 64–128 tokens) tend to excel on concise, fact-based queries, while larger chunks (≈ 512–1,024 tokens) perform better when answers require broader context.

Practical starting points from industry guidance:

- Begin around **250 tokens (~1,000 characters)** and adjust based on evals.
- **Financial Documents**: Approximately 1,800 characters provide the necessary context for complex financial relationships and calculations, while avoiding the 10-20% performance degradation that occurs with chunks exceeding 14,400 characters.

Domain specifics matter: in a finance/SEC filing setting, ~1,800 characters worked well, while ~14,400-character chunks diluted relevance and drove performance drops of around 10–20%.

Metadata enrichment transforms static documents into intelligently searchable assets. Each chunk should be enriched so the agent can filter by what's authoritative and current, not just what's semantically similar. Recommended fields include title, summary, keywords/entities, and machine-generated attributes used for filtering (e.g., document type, created or updated date, owning team or department, approval state). These fields enable hybrid retrieval (combining keyword and AI-powered search for better accuracy) and policy-aware filtering, which ensures results respect business rules such as approvals and ownership.

Implementation Architecture

Building your knowledge agent requires integrating several components, such as vector databases, hybrid search tools, and secure connectors, into a cohesive system that can scale with your organization's needs while maintaining response quality and security standards.

Vector database & hybrid search considerations:

- Pinecone has been benchmarked to achieve low latencies (often under 120 ms at the 95th percentile, meaning almost all queries complete this fast) at tens of millions of vectors, making it a reliable choice when performance and scale matter.
- Weaviate supports true hybrid search (vector + BM25, a proven keyword search algorithm) by running both searches in parallel and fusing results via configurable strategies (e.g., ranked fusion or relative score fusion).
- The choice between them depends on trade-offs: pure vector for raw speed and scale, or hybrid support when exact matching and semantic context both matter.

Integration Architecture: Your agent must interface securely with existing document stores, CRM/ERP systems, and identity/access control. You'll need:

- **API connectors** (pull, push, streaming) to sync content updates,
- **Authentication & authorization** layers respecting your access model (e.g., RBAC, OAuth, SCIM),
- **Audit, logging, and versioning** for traceability and compliance.

Here's how the enhanced architecture extends our Chapter 5 workflow agent:

```
class CustomerKnowledgeAgent(EnhancedTriageAgent):
    def __init__(self):
        super().__init__()
        self.vector_db = PineconeClient(
            api_key=os.environ["PINECONE_API_KEY"],
            environment="production"
        )
        self.knowledge_prompt = self._build_knowledge_prompt()

    def _build_knowledge_prompt(self):
        return ChatPromptTemplate.from_template(
            """
            You are a knowledgeable customer support agent with access to
company documentation.

            Retrieved Context:
            {context_documents}

            Customer Question: {question}
            Customer Tier: {customer_tier}

            Provide a comprehensive answer based on the retrieved
documentation.
            Always cite specific sources and indicate if additional
information is needed.

            Answer:
            """
        )

    async def answer_with_knowledge(self, question, customer_context):
        """Enhanced response using organizational knowledge"""

        # Retrieve relevant documents with filtering
        relevant_docs = self.vector_db.similarity_search(
            query=question,
            k=5,
            filter={
                "department": "customer_success",
                "status": "current",
                "customer_tier": customer_context.get('tier', 'standard')
            }
        )

        # Combine workflow intelligence with knowledge base
        urgency_assessment = self._assess_urgency(question,
customer_context)

        # Generate knowledge-enhanced response
        response = self.knowledge_prompt.invoke({
            "context_documents": self._format_retrieved_docs(relevant_docs),
            "question": question,
            "customer_tier": customer_context.get('tier', 'standard')
        })

        # Include source attribution for transparency
        response_with_sources = {
            "answer": response.content,
            "sources": [doc.metadata for doc in relevant_docs],
            "urgency": urgency_assessment.priority_level.value,
            "routing_recommendation":
self._determine_routing_with_knowledge(
                question, urgency_assessment, relevant_docs
            )
        }

        return response_with_sources

    def _format_retrieved_docs(self, documents):
        """Format retrieved documents for LLM context"""
        formatted = []
        for i, doc in enumerate(documents, 1):
            formatted.append(
                f"Source {i} ({doc.metadata.get('title', 'Unknown')}):\n"
                f"{doc.page_content}\n"
            )
        return "\n".join(formatted)
```

Quality Control and Governance

Enterprise knowledge systems demand rigorous controls to ensure data quality, reliability, and accountability. Each response should include source attribution to ensure auditability and allow user verification.

Accuracy monitoring involves tracking response quality through user feedback, automated evaluation metrics, and periodic human review. Some high-performing systems aim for 85% accuracy rates for factual queries; systems that fail to meet these thresholds require optimization before production deployment.

Content freshness management ensures that a knowledge base accurately reflects the current organizational state. This includes automated updates when source documents change, deprecation handling workflows for outdated information, and conflict resolution when multiple sources provide contradictory user guidance.

The monitoring framework should track key performance indicators that correlate with business value: accuracy, user satisfaction, attribution completeness, and system availability.

Enterprise Success Stories

Uber's Engineering Knowledge Revolution

Like many tech companies, Uber's critical engineering knowledge was trapped in thousands of Slack conversations, making it inaccessible during production incidents or key architectural discussions. To solve this, they implemented an AI-powered engineering copilot using an advanced RAG architecture.

Uber's system now processes 45,000 questions per month, providing engineers with instant access to curated technical documentation and institutional expertise. The business impact has been profound: Uber documented 13,000 engineering hours saved annually—the equivalent of adding six senior engineers to the team. Crucially, the system also improves quality, delivering a 27% increase in acceptable answers and a 60% reduction in incorrect advice compared to standard RAG implementations.

The key insight from Uber's success is its domain-specific focus. By focusing on high-quality engineering content and learning from user interactions, the agent developed a deep understanding of the technical context that a general-purpose system could never achieve.

JPMorgan Chase: Scaling Knowledge to 200,000 Employees

JPMorgan Chase's implementation of its knowledge agent demonstrates knowledge management at an unprecedented scale, serving over 200,000 employees with its "LLM Suite" knowledge platform. For expensive asset management analysts who previously spent hours on manual research, the RAG-enhanced platform now delivers comprehensive insights in minutes.

The documented business impact is transformative. The bank achieved $1.5 billion in annual business value. Beyond savings, AI-powered advisory tools have driven a 20% increase in gross sales and are projected to enable a 50% increase in client roster capacity within five years.

The bank currently operates over 450 proofs of concept, with plans for 1,000+ AI use cases by 2026, suggesting that the knowledge platform serves as foundational infrastructure for broader AI transformation. This scaling approach, which involves building robust knowledge capabilities first and then expanding use cases, represents a repeatable pattern for achieving enterprise AI success.

Goldman Sachs: Projecting Transformational Productivity

Goldman Sachs' AI Assistant platform, currently serving 10,000+ employees with company-wide expansion planned for 2025, illustrates the next evolution of enterprise knowledge systems. The investment bank expects 3-4x productivity gains through agentic AI integration that combines institutional knowledge with specialized financial workflows.

The platform demonstrates how knowledge systems can move beyond information retrieval to actively create work products. This represents a fundamental shift from knowledge access to knowledge application. The system not only finds relevant information but also uses it to generate initial drafts, analysis frameworks, and implementation approaches.

Goldman Sachs' strategic vision envisions AI systems functioning as "seasoned Goldman employees" within 3-5 years, fundamentally transforming trading and investment banking operations through integration with proprietary data and specialized financial workflows. This ambition reflects confidence in knowledge systems as a foundation technology that can scale across diverse business functions while maintaining the precision and expertise that defines the firm's competitive position.

The Pattern of Success

These successful implementations share a common DNA. They are driven by executive sponsorship that guarantees resources, built on the knowledge of domain experts who ensure content quality, and launched using a phased approach that starts with a focused pilot to prove value before scaling. Critically, they are treated as living systems, with continuous optimization through user feedback and performance monitoring, ensuring they evolve and maintain high accuracy over time.

Business Impact and ROI from Knowledge Systems

Implementing a knowledge agent can yield compounding value across operations, talent, and strategic layers, although exact returns depend heavily on context, baseline processes, and scale.

Productivity gains manifest via reduced search time, fewer context switches, and faster decision support. In many knowledge management initiatives, organizations report that employees spend a non-trivial portion of their day (e.g., multiple hours weekly) locating information. Some estimates suggest that as much as 8 hours per week is spent searching for information across systems and that effective KM systems can reduce this burden by 30-35%.

For talent acceleration, knowledge agents help new hires ramp more quickly by surfacing institutional knowledge and reducing reliance on ad hoc mentoring.

The financial case for knowledge agents is often cast as "high ROI over time," especially when the system is reused across domains and evolves. While many early claims about KM ROI were speculative, the key to achieving a strong return is to approach the investment realistically. As the *Harvard Business Review* notes, success depends on proper planning. This means building in budget contingencies for infrastructure scaling and data quality efforts. Most importantly, view this not as a one-off project, but as a foundational platform investment that will lower the cost and accelerate the deployment of all future AI initiatives across your enterprise.

Implementation Challenges and Success Strategies

The stark reality of enterprise RAG implementation demands strategic attention: 72% of deployments fail within the first year, with infrastructure overruns being the primary killer.

During periods of market volatility, a finance firm's RAG system suffered infrastructure scaling failures, forcing $200,000 in emergency vector database capacity spend and 14 hours of downtime in critical trading windows. The incident led to a complete migration toward a hybrid retrieval approach.

Accuracy shortfalls can also lead to failures. Systems that skip rigorous document preparation, domain-grounded evaluation, and human review struggle to meet enterprise accuracy expectations. Research on knowledge quality and human-in-the-loop practices highlights the importance of expert curation, periodic human review, and feedback loops in maintaining factuality and minimizing drift.

Integration complexity is another challenge that businesses must address. Even the strongest prototypes can stall when connecting to identity, security, and legacy content systems. Consistent guidance from transformation literature: treat integration, access control, auditability, and change management as first-class workstreams, not afterthoughts.

The organizations that achieve breakthrough business results consistently demonstrate a commitment to four key principles:

1. **Executive Sponsorship:** Successful projects are championed by senior leaders who secure resources, ensure cross-functional alignment, and remove the inevitable organizational roadblocks that arise during implementation.
2. **Domain Expert Involvement:** Successful projects are a partnership between AI experts and your company's own subject matter experts. Involving domain experts in curating knowledge sources and validating agent responses is the only way to ensure the system is accurate, relevant, and trusted by users.
3. **User-Centric Design:** The best systems are built with, not for, their users. Integrating systematic user feedback loops and treating the agent as an internal product that evolves based on user needs is crucial for driving adoption and ensuring the solution is solving the right problems.
4. **Focus on Workflow Redesign:** As McKinsey's research on the state of AI makes clear, enterprise-level impact only materializes when you restructure processes *around* the agent's new capabilities, rather than simply bolting new technology onto old ways of working.

Conclusion: Building Institutional Intelligence

We have evolved our agent from a workflow orchestrator into a knowledge-enabled strategist. While the agent from Chapter 5 provided a foundation for coordinating tasks, a knowledge agent adds access to decades of accumulated expertise. It transcends the limits of old search systems by understanding semantic meaning, creating a system that provides contextual intelligence, not just retrieved information.

This capability is a true competitive moat. AI technology may be a commodity, but your organization's proprietary knowledge is not. An effective knowledge agent turns this unique asset into a source of superior decision-making and operational speed.

A robust knowledge agent is the prerequisite for the next level of AI maturity.

In the next chapter, we will explore how multiple specialized agents can collaborate, using this shared institutional memory to tackle complex, multi-faceted business challenges.

References:

- Various Survey Statistics: Workers Spend Too Much Time Searching for Information
- Vector search in Azure AI Search | Microsoft Learn
- Out-of-Domain Semantics to the Rescue! Zero-Shot Hybrid Retrieval Models
- Efficient Knowledge Graph Accuracy Evaluation
- Evaluating Chunking Strategies for Retrieval
- Rethinking Chunk Size For Long-Document Retrieval: A Multi-Dataset Analysis
- Chunking for RAG: best practices
- Long-Context Isn't All You Need: Impact of Retrieval and Chunking on Finance RAG
- RAG chunk enrichment phase | Microsoft Learn
- February Release: Performance at Scale, Predictability, and Control | Pinecone
- Hybrid search | Weaviate Documentation
- Knowledge Management ROI: Here's Why You Should Invest in Your Organizational Knowledge
- What's Your Return on Knowledge? | Harvard Business Review
- Can return on investment in knowledge management initiatives in organizations be measured? Aslib Journal of Information Management
- Uber's Genie Achieves Near-Human Precision with Enhanced Agentic RAG
- Genie: Uber's AI-Powered Copilot for Efficient Incident Management
- JPMorgan Chase launches AI assistant and revolutionizes banking operations
- Case Study: How JPMorgan Chase is Revolutionizing Banking Through AI

- JPMorgan Chase aims to create $1.5 billion in value with AI by year-end
- Goldman Sachs rolls out an AI assistant for its employees as artificial intelligence sweeps Wall Street
- Goldman Sachs is piloting its first autonomous coder in major AI milestone for Wall Street
- Why 72% of Enterprise RAG Implementations Fail in the First Year—and How to Avoid the Same Fate
- The Hidden Cost Crisis: Why 73% of Enterprise RAG Systems Are Hemorrhaging Money and How EraRAG Changes Everything
- Seven Failure Points When Engineering a Retrieval Augmented Generation System
- Why Most RAG Systems Fail in Production (and How to Fix Them) | by Koushik Reddy | Aug, 2025 | Medium
- Human-in-the-Loop Approach: Bridging AI & Human Expertise
- The State of AI How organizations are rewiring to capture value (McKinsey)

CHAPTER 7

From Single Agent to Swarm

The knowledge agent we built in Chapter 6 represents a powerful business asset. With access to institutional memory, it can provide substantive guidance based on its accumulated expertise. Yet even this sophisticated system has a critical limitation: it operates as a specialist in a world that demands a team of experts.

In the real world, enterprise challenges rarely present themselves as isolated tickets.

Imagine a SaaS provider facing a critical escalation:

- Adoption rates are falling.
- A major contract renewal is due for renewal.
- Integration with a compliance system is stalled.
- The finance team notices irregular payment patterns.
- Customer support logs show rising frustration.

Each issue is important in its own right. But in practice, issues often unfold at the same time. A single knowledge agent can retrieve documentation and provide accurate answers in isolation, but it cannot simultaneously analyze usage trends, financial risk, relationship sentiment, and technical status. Nor can it ensure that actions taken in one area (e.g., adjusting billing terms) align with what's happening in another (e.g., resolving adoption problems).

Enterprise customer success resembles a symphony rather than a solo performance. The knowledge agent shines like a virtuoso, yet without the orchestra, the depth and resonance are incomplete.

True customer success requires multiple specialists, including those in billing, technical support, account management, and product usage, all working in coordinated harmony.

With agentic systems, we must not make the mistake of replacing human silos with agentic silos. Siloes must be collapsed through multi-agent systems, often called "agent swarms". The leap from specialization to orchestration is the core architectural shift required for scaling AI to drive customer success.

This architecture eliminates the trade-off between narrow expertise and comprehensive awareness. Instead of a single generalist agent, businesses deploy a team of specialized agents, each an expert in its domain, that collaborate under the direction of an intelligent orchestrator.

Multi-Agent Coordination Patterns

To deploy multi-agent systems effectively, executives must understand a few canonical coordination patterns. These patterns enable you to map business complexity to architectural simplicity.

The Architecture of Collaboration

Multi-agent systems collaborate using four primary patterns, each designed for a specific type of business problem. Choosing the right pattern is a critical strategic decision that strikes a balance between complexity and business value.

1. **Sequential Handoffs:** For predictable, step-by-step processes. An inquiry is passed through a chain of specialist agents in a predetermined sequence, each step building upon the previous one. This is ideal for standardized workflows such as customer onboarding.
2. **Parallel Processing:** For speed and comprehensive analysis. Multiple agents work on different facets of a problem simultaneously: one pulls financial data while another analyzes support history. This reduces the time needed to resolve complex issues.
3. **Hierarchical Coordination:** For dynamic, multi-faceted problems. A "manager" agent directs and coordinates the work of specialized sub-agents, delegating tasks and synthesizing their findings to ensure effective collaboration. This provides centralized oversight for complex and evolving situations.
4. **Peer Collaboration:** For sophisticated problem-solving. Specialized agents consult with one another to share insights and enhance decision quality. For example, a "churn prediction" agent might query a "usage data" agent to validate its reasoning, ensuring a more accurate final assessment.

Pattern	Description	Best Use Cases
Sequential Handoffs	Inquiry flows through a fixed chain (triage → knowledge → action)	Standardized workflows (e.g. billing escalations)
Parallel Processing	Agents analyze distinct problem facets simultaneously	Complex requests requiring cross-domain insight
Hierarchical Coordination	A central "master" agent delegates tasks to specialized sub-agents	Dynamic work allocation in large-scale operations
Peer Collaboration	Agents share viewpoints, challenge each other, reach consensus	Highly ambiguous or contested scenarios

Effective swarms combine these modes flexibly. E.g., start with parallel analysis, then converge via a coordinator or consensus mechanism.

Communication Protocols: The Language of a High-Performing Team

A team of brilliant specialists is ineffective if they cannot communicate. For a multi-agent system to function as a cohesive unit, it needs a shared language and rules of engagement that ensure scalability, coherence, and reliability.

- **Event-driven messaging** (publish/subscribe): Instead of relying on direct, one-to-one calls that can create bottlenecks, the agents communicate through a central message board. One agent "publishes" an update (e.g., "Customer context gathered"), and other relevant agents "subscribe" to that information to inform their next action. This event-driven architecture decouples the agents, allowing the system to scale massively without collapsing under its own weight.
- **Layered context architectures**: To ensure a seamless customer experience, this communication is structured in layers. Each agent understands the context of its immediate task, the overall customer session, and the system-wide strategic goals. This prevents the "left hand not knowing what the right hand is doing" and ensures the customer receives a single, coherent response.
- **Conflict resolution protocols**: When faced with contradictory recommendations, agents can enter a consensus round or dynamically transfer leadership to a third agent to break the deadlock, ensuring the best possible action is taken.
- **Enforcement Agents**: In safety-sensitive systems, embedding oversight agents (i.e., "enforcement agents") helps monitor behavior, detect misalignment, and intervene in real time. (This is a subject of recent academic work.)

Recent benchmarks demonstrate that multi-agent collaboration can increase end-to-end goal success rates by up to 70% compared to single-agent approaches for certain enterprise tasks, provided that communication and coordination protocols are well-designed and effective.

Specialized Agent Roles

Multi-agent systems outperform monolithic AI for the same reason a team of human specialists (such as a lawyer, a marketer, and an engineer) outperforms a single generalist on complex problems. By assigning specific roles, each agent develops deep expertise in its domain. This architectural pattern is a proven best practice for boosting the accuracy and capability of complex AI systems. A 2025 arXiv paper on the Model Context Protocol (MCP) for multi-agent systems confirms that replacing highly specialized agents with more general-purpose agents reduced peak performance by 31.7%.

In our Customer Success Swarm, we would deploy a team of five core specialists:

1. **The Triage Agent (The Front Door):** This agent extends the capabilities from Chapter 5. It serves as an intelligent entry point, assessing the initial request to determine which other agents need to be involved and in what sequence.

2. **The Knowledge Agent (The Corporate Memory):** Leveraging the RAG architecture from Chapter 6, this agent is the swarm's expert on all internal institutional knowledge, providing historical context and documented precedents on demand.

3. **The Research Agent (The Market Analyst):** This agent complements the Knowledge Agent by gathering real-time, *external* information. It monitors market trends, competitive intelligence, or news that might impact the customer.

4. **The Action Agent (The Executor):** This agent serves as the "hands" of the swarm. It is responsible for coordinating and executing tasks across your actual business systems, such as updating a CRM, creating a support ticket, or processing a payment.

5. **The Follow-up Agent (The Quality Controller):** This agent closes the loop. It monitors the outcomes of the other agents' actions, verifies that tasks were completed successfully, and tracks customer satisfaction to help the swarm learn and improve over time.

The Coordinator Agent - The Master Conductor

The Coordinator Agent is the most critical component of a multi-agent system. Like a symphony conductor, its role is not to play an instrument but to orchestrate the entire team of specialized agents, transforming their individual actions into a single, unified customer success outcome.

Intelligence & Routing Strategy

Unlike a static workflow engine that follows a predetermined path, an intelligent coordinator makes three critical decisions in real-time to adapt to any situation:

1. **Dynamic agent activation**: Instead of fixed workflows, the coordinator determines which agents to invoke (and when) based on customer tier, issue complexity, and risk indicators.

2. **Capacity-aware load balancing**: By tracking agent utilization and response times, the coordinator avoids bottlenecks and can reallocate or deprioritize less urgent tasks.

3. **Predictive routing**: Machine learning models, trained on past cases, anticipate which agents will be needed and pre-route requests to minimize latency.

Here's how advanced coordination logic operates in practice:

```
class CustomerSuccessCoordinator:
    def __init__(self):
        self.agents = {
            'triage': TriageAgent(),
            'knowledge': KnowledgeAgent(),
            'research': ResearchAgent(),
            'financial': FinancialHealthAgent(),
            'relationship': RelationshipAgent(),
            'action': ActionAgent(),
            'followup': FollowupAgent()
        }
        self.workflow_engine = WorkflowEngine()
        self.context_manager = ContextManager()

    async def process_customer_issue(self, customer_data,
issue_description):
        # Initialize coordination context
        context = self.context_manager.create_session(customer_data)

        # Initial triage with coordination planning
        triage_result = await
self.agents['triage'].assess_with_coordination(
            customer_data, issue_description, context
        )

        # Build dynamic workflow based on complexity and customer tier
        coordination_pattern = self._determine_coordination_pattern(
            triage_result, customer_data
        )

        # Execute coordinated response with parallel and sequential phases
        if coordination_pattern.requires_parallel_analysis:
            parallel_results = await self._execute_parallel_analysis(
                coordination_pattern, context
            )
            context.update_with_analysis(parallel_results)

        # Sequential coordination for actions requiring specific order
        final_results = await self._execute_sequential_actions(
            coordination_pattern, context
        )

        # Comprehensive follow-up coordination
        await self._coordinate_followup(final_results, context)

        return self._generate_comprehensive_response(context, final_results)

    def _determine_coordination_pattern(self, triage_result, customer_data):
        """Advanced logic for determining optimal agent coordination"""
        pattern = CoordinationPattern()

        # Enterprise customers get comprehensive coordination
        if customer_data.tier == 'enterprise':
            pattern.add_parallel_agents(['financial', 'relationship',
'research'])
            pattern.add_sequential_phase(['knowledge', 'action'])
            pattern.escalation_threshold = 'low'

        # High complexity issues require specialized coordination
        if triage_result.complexity_score > 7:
            pattern.add_collaboration_group(['knowledge', 'research'])
            pattern.enable_consensus_mechanism()

        # Churn risk triggers proactive coordination
        if triage_result.churn_indicators:
            pattern.add_priority_agent('relationship')
            pattern.enable_real_time_monitoring()

        return pattern
```

State Management & Governance

A team of autonomous agents, however specialized, risks becoming a fragmented battalion working at cross-purposes without a strong framework for coordination and governance. To transform them into a unified operating instrument, the coordinator agent enforces three critical principles that ensure cohesion, accountability, and safety.

1. **Consistent context store (Single Source of Truth)**: All agents in the swarm access and update a shared, consistent context store like a living digital file on the customer. This prevents agents from acting on conflicting or outdated information, ensuring that every part of the system operates from the same playbook.
2. **Audit logging and traceability**: Every decision, handoff, and action taken by any agent is logged in an immutable audit trail. For governance, compliance, and performance analysis, this is a non-negotiable requirement. It transforms the agent's work from a "black box" into a fully auditable process.
3. **Human escalation gating**: An agent's most important skill is knowing the limits of its own knowledge. The coordinator is programmed with clear protocols to escalate an issue to a human operator whenever confidence is low, a conflict cannot be resolved, or the situation requires a level of nuance that only a person can provide.

In short, the coordinator turns a collection of agents into a unified operating instrument — not a fragmented battalion.

Technical Implementation of Multi-Agent Coordination

We have already explored coordination patterns at a high level earlier. Now we will turn to the technical foundation that makes them possible. For a business executive, understanding the core architectural principles is not so much about knowing the code as it is about ensuring your technical teams are building a system that is scalable, reliable, and secure.

Infrastructure Architecture for Production Deployment

Instead of building one huge, monolithic application, a modern agent swarm is built using a microservices architecture. This architecture provides immense scalability and resilience. If the business need for sales-related agents suddenly triples, your team can scale up just that one service without touching the rest of the system. If the Knowledge Agent encounters an error, it doesn't bring down the entire triage operation. This model, often managed by platforms like Kubernetes, is the globally accepted standard for building scalable, high-availability systems.

In a multi-agent swarm, a service mesh serves as a shared communication layer, enabling agents to exchange information securely and transparently without requiring each agent to have its own custom messaging system. Advanced service mesh setups can automatically handle encryption, manage traffic between agents, and monitor performance to ensure optimal operation. This keeps the swarm coordinated and efficient, while still allowing each agent to remain independent and evolve freely.

Database and State Management Patterns

Distributed state management represents one of the most critical technical challenges in multi-agent implementation. Each agent requires access to customer context while maintaining its specialized domain knowledge. However, traditional centralized databases create bottlenecks that constrain coordination performance.

Event sourcing architectures enable agents to maintain consistent views of customer state while supporting independent operation. Instead of all agents reading and writing to the same database, they "publish" updates and "subscribe" to the streams of information they require.

CQRS (Command Query Responsibility Segregation) patterns separate read and write operations to optimize performance for different agent coordination scenarios. Agents requiring real-time customer context use optimized read models, while agents making state changes use write models designed for consistency and audit requirements.

Message Queuing and Communication Protocols

Enterprise message bus implementation using platforms like Apache Kafka or Azure Service Bus provides the communication backbone for agent coordination. They make sure messages are delivered, ordered correctly, and can be replayed if something fails. This way, the agents don't lose coordination.

Choosing between synchronous and asynchronous communication affects how the swarm behaves: synchronous provides fast responses but can spread failures across agents. While asynchronous is more resilient, it requires extra tracking to keep workflows aligned.

Dead letter queue management handles coordination failures gracefully. Dead letter queues catch messages that can't be processed, sending them for review or retry. This prevents failures from spreading through the swarm and often helps reveal deeper system issues.

Performance Optimization and Scaling Strategies

Instead of scaling based on each agent's resource use, multi-agent systems work better when they **auto-scale based on coordination load**, such as conversation complexity, demand for specialists, or backlog. This is common in microservice architectures, but swarm systems tune it for coordination needs.

Caching shared context (like customer state, knowledge base answers, or analysis results) speeds things up by avoiding repeated work. The challenge is maintaining consistent caches across agents. With smart strategies, caching can cut coordination overhead and boost performance by up to 66%.

Circuit breaker patterns prevent coordination failures from cascading across agent networks. If a specialist agent goes down, the swarm doesn't collapse; instead, it continues with reduced functionality, keeping service running while the issue is fixed.

Conclusion: The Future of Customer Success

The transition from a single-agent paradigm to orchestrated swarms is surely not going to be an ordinary incremental step in industrial history. This will redefine the operating model of customer success. It enables enterprises to deliver expert-level service at scale by collapsing functional silos into seamless, AI-coordinated workflows.

But executives must not be seduced by flashy ROI claims or technical jargon. Success depends on a handful of disciplines working together.

Organizations that achieve lasting results build on solid architectural foundations, ensuring scalability and reliability from the outset. They apply rigorous measurement discipline, treating ROI tracking and performance monitoring as central to the initiative, not afterthoughts. They embed governance and escalation protocols that safeguard against coordination failures and maintain human oversight. They advance through phased, value-driven deployment, resisting the temptation to scale prematurely. And they cultivate cultural alignment, training teams to work with agent swarms as collaborators rather than treating them as opaque automation tools.

Gartner expects agentic AI features to be present in a third of enterprise applications by 2028, indicating that this capability will transition from a competitive advantage to a baseline expectation. Meanwhile, nearly half of all agentic projects may fail if value isn't clearly managed and communicated.

The network effects of multi-agent learning create sustainable competitive advantages as coordination patterns are optimized based on successful outcomes and customer feedback. Organizations with longer deployments will accumulate coordination intelligence, enabling superior performance compared to later adopters attempting to replicate similar capabilities.

For customer success to become a strategic differentiator in the age of AI, organizations must master not only agents but agent orchestration. The companies that crack that architecture and governance challenge will outpace rivals in retention, expansion, and scalable excellence.

References:

- Enforcement Agents: Enhancing Accountability and Resilience in Multi-Agent AI Frameworks
- Towards Effective GenAI Multi-Agent Collaboration: Design and Evaluation for Enterprise Applications
- Advancing Multi-Agent Systems Through Model Context Protocol: Architecture, Implementation, and Applications
- Enforcement Agents: Enhancing Accountability and Resilience in Multi-Agent AI Frameworks
- Event Sourcing pattern | Microsoft Azure Learn
- Event Sourcing - Martin Fowler
- Multi-Agent Safety Verification using Symmetry Transformations
- Intelligent Agents in AI Really Can Work Alone. Here's How.
- Over 40% of agentic AI projects will be scrapped by 2027, Gartner says

CHAPTER 8

Architecture that Scales

Executives rarely reject good business ideas. They reject ideas that cannot survive a cost-benefit analysis, a risk review, or those that can't scale. That is why the most important step in your AI agent journey is the shift from a "working demo" to a production-ready, value-creating asset. A demo shows potential. An asset produces measurable, repeatable, and valuable business outcomes under real-world conditions: impatient users, messy data, disparate IT systems, security-exacting audits, and cost pressures.

The Production Mindset: Crossing the Chasm from Prototype to Asset

Production readiness rests on four pillars that translate directly into executive concerns.

1. **Reliability** means the system works when customers and employees use it. That requires 24/7 availability, regular health checks, and automated failover so the system does not experience incidents before they cause revenue or reputational damage.
2. **Scalability** means the system can handle growth without incurring runaway expenses, allowing you to achieve elasticity and throughput without budget shock.
3. **Security** means adopting a zero-trust posture with strong identity and access management, encryption, and continuous monitoring and alerting to reduce the risk of becoming the next breach headline.
4. **Maintainability** means models, prompts, and integrations can be updated without disrupting business operations.

These pillars separate experiments from assets.

The stakes have never been higher. While the enterprise AI market is projected to grow from $97.2 billion in 2025 to over $229.3 billion by 2030, the Boston Consulting Group's 2024 research reveals a sobering reality: 74% of companies struggle to achieve and scale value from their AI initiatives. Yet for the organizations that get it right, the returns are transformative.

McKinsey reports that CEO oversight of AI governance correlates most strongly with the bottom-line impact, yet only 28% of organizations have implemented this structure.

The bottom line is that AI's potential value only matters for your company if your systems can remain online, stay secure, and scale at a cost profile that a CFO deemed acceptable.

Core Architectural Decisions and Strategic Trade-offs

Architecture is not a technical indulgence. It is a financial strategy expressed in systems. The architectural choices you make determine how fast you can ship, how safely you can scale, and how predictably you can budget. Below are the decisions that matter most to executives, as each creates a tangible trade-off among cost, speed, flexibility, and risk.

Infrastructure: Serverless vs. Containers

Think of serverless like a courier service. You pay per pick-up. There is almost no waiting to get started, and the provider optimizes routes for you. This suits spiky, event-driven work such as classification tasks, message triage, and short-lived tool calls. The benefits include speed and a consumption model that aligns costs to usage.

Compared to containers, serverless gives you less control over the underlying infrastructure and can create a form of "soft lock-in," since you are bound by the provider's runtime limits, features, and pricing model. Cloud guidance reinforces the fact that being serverless means you don't have to spend time forecasting how much computing power you'll need in advance. The system automatically scales resources up or down in response to changing demand.

However, engineering teams must still manage function runtime and design patterns that avoid hidden charges such as idle polling. Idle polling is like asking, "Are we there yet?" over and over, even when nothing has changed. The computer continually checks for tasks to perform, rather than waiting quietly until needed, which consumes computing power and incurs costs.

Containers are like owning a fleet. You decide what to buy, how to maintain it, and where it goes. The benefit is control: you can tune performance, enforce consistent environments, and deploy across clouds or on-premises. The trade-off is higher overhead, requiring orchestration, security patching, and cost management for persistent workloads.

The market's direction is clear. Container and Kubernetes adoption is now mainstream, with the latest CNCF survey reporting that approximately 91 percent of organizations use containers in production. That ubiquity raises expectations, as cost and security responsibilities fall squarely on the enterprise.

Executive Decision-Making Matrix for executives.

If you need fast, event-driven pilots with unpredictable demand, serverless matches costs to usage and reduces time to value. For steady, high-throughput workloads with multiple services and custom runtimes, containers offer the control and portability that pay off over time. Cloud providers echo this guidance: choose managed serverless for stateless microservices, and move to Kubernetes when you need fine-grained scheduling, custom networking, or coordination across services."

Factor	Serverless	Containers
Time to market	Days to weeks	Weeks to months
Cost model	Pay-per-use (variable)	Fixed + variable
Control	Limited customization	Full control
Best for	Event-driven, variable load	Steady, high throughput
Lock-in risk	Higher (provider-specific)	Lower (portable)

Data: From Static Files to Real-Time Pipelines

Prototypes often connect retrieval systems to static documents or batch snapshots, which is enough to answer common questions. Production agents need to detect changes and act quickly, requiring streaming, change-data-capture, or event hubs that deliver new data in real-time.

Confluent's 2025 Data Streaming Report notes that 89% of IT leaders view data streaming platforms as critical or important to data goals, and 44% report five-times ROI from streaming investments. The strategic point is not the vendor but the principle: time-sensitive decisions demand time-sensitive data, which calls for investment in pipelines, governance, and operations beyond a basic RAG index.

Streaming requires schema management, observability, and replay strategies, and it shifts ownership of data quality. Operations teams that once managed daily batches must now sustain 24/7 feeds. That is the price of faster loop times — often justified for customer service, fraud detection, inventory, or risk use cases where minutes matter. Without this investment, you limit how far agents can safely automate.

Integration: The "Last Mile" Problem

The fastest way to stall an agent's initiative is to underestimate the importance of integration. Agents create value only when they can read and write to systems of record. Enterprises now run hundreds of applications — MuleSoft reports an average of 897 per organization, with 95% of IT leaders citing integration as a barrier to AI adoption. That complexity is why integration often consumes the majority of the effort and delivers most of the value. Cutting corners here leads to brittle automations, data drift, and security gaps that wipe out ROI.

What should an executive watch?

- **Permissions:** Write access without fine-grained scopes creates risk, while read-only pilots cannot close loops.
- **Backlog:** Timelines hinge on CRM, ERP, ticketing, billing, and data platform access — not agent code.
- **Reuse:** Build APIs and event streams once, then spread the value across multiple agents.

Benchmark data shows integration debt is the systemic bottleneck to AI scale. Treat integration as a platform, not a project.

Security: From Open Lab to Digital Fortress

Prototype environments can tolerate shortcuts. Production cannot. The **zero-trust** approach, as defined by NIST, shifts defenses from static network perimeters toward identity, device health, and continuous authorization. It treats the network as hostile, enforces the principle of least privilege, and verifies every access. This model is essential once agents handle sensitive workflows.

Verizon's DBIR reveals that credential abuse is a dominant pattern in web-application breaches. In the "Basic Web Application Attacks" category, 88% of breaches involved the use of stolen credentials. The takeaway is clear: prioritize identity, secret management, and audit trails before expanding the scope.

Cost realism matters. IBM reports the average global breach at $4.44 million. Breaches that span multiple environments are even more expensive, averaging $5.05 million, and in the US, the figure exceeds $10 million. The most cost-effective breach is the one prevented through identity controls, encryption, and observability. In practice: follow CISA's zero-trust maturity model, enforce strong authentication, keep credentials out of logs and prompts, and track agent actions with immutable audit trails.

The Real Costs

There is no fixed 'cost of an agent'; cost follows ambition. Think in tiers aligned to scope, integrations, and rigor. The figures below represent planning ranges derived from current market rates for cloud services, commercial tools, and typical engineering efforts. Actual numbers may vary by region, vendor, and internal capabilities, but these estimates provide informed guidance.

Tier 1: The High-Value Pilot

Scope: A Minimum Viable Agent focused on a narrow, high-pain use case, such as email triage or knowledge retrieval for a single team. Integrations are usually limited to one or two systems, often read-heavy with staged write-backs.

One-time investment: about $25,000 to $60,000 for configuration, integration work, basic observability, and security hardening.

Recurring run rate: about $500 to $2,500 per month for model calls, serverless compute, vector stores, and monitoring.

Business result: Reduction in queue times, faster response quality, and measurable deflection of tickets. OSF HealthCare realized $2.4 million ROI in the first year from their AI virtual assistant "Clare," which provides 24/7 patient support and significantly reduced call center volume.

Tier 2: The Departmental Solution

Scope: A multi-agent pattern that coordinates triage, knowledge, research, and action within a core function such as Customer Success. It integrates with three to five systems, adopts event-driven patterns, and completes loops with controlled write access.

One-time investment: about $75,000 to $250,000 to deliver orchestration, real-time data, identity, and observability that supports handoffs.

Recurring run rate: about $3,000 to $20,000 per month for model usage, containers, or mixed serverless, streaming infrastructure, vector indices, and logging.

Business result: Lower escalations and faster resolutions can drive measurable reductions in churn. Even a **five per cent churn reduction** compounds quickly given customer lifetime values. Integration discipline matters here.

Tier 3: The Enterprise Platform

Scope: A company-wide capability built around an AI Center of Excellence. Multiple agents serve several functions, supported by a hardened zero-trust posture, shared APIs, and streaming data backbones.

One-time investment: about $500,000 and above for the platform, unified identity, standardized monitoring, and industrialized MLOps.

Recurring run rate: about $50,000 per month and up for compute, data platforms, observability, and a small reliability crew.

Business result: Durable productivity lift across functions, new product features, and the ability to create net-new revenue models. The upside exists, but so do costs if governance is weak.

Gartner has warned that at least 30% of generative AI projects will be abandoned after proof of concept, often due to poor data quality, weak risk controls, rising costs, or unclear business value. The remedy is to treat the platform as a strategic asset, managed with a clear portfolio and defined stages and gates.

A false economy often emerges between Tiers 1 and 2. Skimping on integration, identity, and observability to 'save now' creates costly rework when scaling to Tier 3.

Cloud cost headwinds also demand early discipline. Flexera's 2025 State of the Cloud report states that 84 percent of organizations struggle to manage cloud spend. The FinOps community reports similar patterns and advocates for a cross-functional approach to enhance visibility and align costs with value, particularly as AI workloads continue to expand.

As such, build cost governance into your architecture from day one.

CAPEX vs. OPEX in the three-tier model

Tier	One-time focus (CAPEX-like)	Ongoing focus (OPEX)
Pilot	Quick integrations, baseline controls, lightweight monitoring	Model calls, serverless compute, basic logs
Department	Orchestration, events, identity and secrets, deeper observability	Mixed compute, streaming, vector indices, SRE throttles
Enterprise	Shared APIs, zero-trust, MLOps, platform reliability	Platform teams, model cost management, enterprise telemetry

The Reality of Timelines

Timelines scale with ambition and with the maturity of data, integrations, and governance.

- **Tier 1 Pilot (4–8 weeks):** The critical path is not model choice but clean data access and clear success metrics. Use the first two weeks for discovery and environment hardening, then deliver a controlled pilot to one team before expanding it to the rest of the teams.
- **Tier 2 Departmental (3–6 months):** Effort shifts to integration and orchestration. Pilots move from read-only to read-write workflows with guardrails, supported by an event fabric and extended identity scopes. The main challenge is coordination with business owners and security reviewers.

- **Tier 3 Enterprise (12–18 months):** This is a strategic program, not a tool purchase. The goal is to achieve a reusable capability that serves multiple functions, underpinned by shared APIs, data products, and common controls.

Expect portfolio governance, standardization of prompts and patterns, and reliability targets with on-call rotations. Most proof-of-concepts stall here, not due to a lack of model performance, but because organizations underestimate the integration and governance challenges. Independent analysts have noted significant abandonment rates for GenAI projects when data quality, risk controls, and cost management are weak.

Do not scale pilots until your foundations support scale.

POC vs. Production at a glance

Dimension	POC goal	Production requirement
Reliability	Works for demo users	Automated failover, SLOs, incident runbooks
Scalability	Handles a handful of flows	Elastic scale with cost guardrails and capacity forecasts
Security	Basic access control	Zero-trust identity, encryption in transit and at rest, audit trails
Maintainability	Manual tweaks acceptable	Versioned prompts, models, configs, and rollout automation

A simple timeline ladder

Phase	Typical duration	Executive checkpoint
Pilot	4–8 weeks	Pain point solved, operator feedback, early cost profile
Expansion	3–6 months	Closed-loop workflows, write access with guardrails, first ROI
Platform	12–18 months	Shared services, zero-trust posture, portfolio and SLOs

Accelerating Time-to-Value with Agile

You can lower cost and risk by sequencing ambition. Begin with a Minimum Viable Agent that tackles a specific, high-pain problem. Make it safe, observable, and measurable. Use the savings and goodwill from that success to fund the next agent. The flywheel is simple: prove value in one workflow, expand integrations and users, standardize patterns and controls, then institutionalize as a platform.

Teams often overlook a second accelerator. Align architectural choices with workload patterns. Use serverless for bursty, event-driven tasks so you only pay for what runs. Shift predictable, high-throughput workloads into containers and negotiate committed use discounts. This discipline avoids spending shocks that derail expansion. Cloud providers and the FinOps community consistently advise users to adopt a consumption-based model, right-size resources, and maintain chargeback or showback so that business owners can see costs tied directly to the delivered value.

Integration discipline is the third accelerator.

Avoid point-to-point connections for every new agent. Instead, establish a small set of reusable integration products, such as customer profile APIs, billing write-backs, ticketing actions, and event topics. Treat integrations as products to shorten future builds and strengthen security and observability.

Security and compliance should be design inputs, not afterthoughts. Apply NIST zero-trust principles early: require strong authentication, keep secrets out of prompts and logs, and automate audits and approvals for write operations. Building this way accelerates progress by preventing late-stage surprises.

Conclusion

There is no universal price tag for an AI agent. Cost scales with ambition, scope, and architectural rigor. Pilots are a low-cost way to prove value against specific pain points. Departmental solutions require orchestration, events, identity, and observability, which necessitate larger budgets. Enterprise platforms are multi-quarter programs that deliver shared capabilities and governance across multiple quarters. These distinctions shape how capital is allocated and how return is measured.

Align ambition with strategy, then budget accordingly. Treat integration, identity, and observability reusable platform work. Match workload patterns to cost profiles with serverless and containers. Plan zero-trust controls and audits from the start to enable safe expansion. Keep a disciplined portfolio: retire pilots that do not deliver, scale those that do.

The leaders will not be those with flashy demos, but those who turn demos into durable assets — reliable, scalable, secure, and maintainable. Build with those pillars, and you create a system that compounds value quarter after quarter.

References:

- AI Adoption in 2024: 74% of Companies Struggle to Achieve and Scale Value | BCG
- Enterprise AI Market - Share, Trends & Size 2025 - 2030
- The State of AI: How organizations are rewiring to capture value (McKinsey)
- Cost of a Data Breach 2025 | IBM
- Verizon: 2025 Data Breach Investigations Report
- CNCF: Annual Survey 2024
- Case Studies in AI-Driven Customer Retention: Success Stories from SaaS, eCommerce, and Subscription Services - SuperAGI
- AWS and Google Cloud guidance on serverless vs. container trade-offs
- Data Streaming Report 2025 | Confluent
- 2025 Connectivity Benchmark Report | Mulesoft
- Cost Optimization - AWS Well-Architected Framework
- Gartner: 30% of Gen AI Projects Will Be Abandoned
- Flexera: State of the Cloud 2025
- State of FinOps: 2025 Report
- NIST SP 800-207 and 207A for zero-trust architecture guidance

CHAPTER 9

Governance, Guardrails, and Ethics

Introduction: The High Cost of Ungoverned AI

The difference between a celebrated AI launch and a reputational crisis is rarely the quality of your AI algorithms. It is AI governance. The best-performing organizations treat governance as the operating system for their AI programs. Governance defines who decides project scope and design, what gets logged, how issues get escalated, and when to stop a rollout. It is not red tape. It is the discipline that allows you to move fast without breaking things that matter.

The risk profile of AI enterprise platforms is real and quantifiable. We observed in the previous chapter that the average global cost of a data breach is now approximately $4.44 million. In the United States, it exceeds $10 million. Breaches become increasingly complex, and AI is now a part of both businesses' defensive and offensive landscapes. These figures provide some indication as to why boards require proof that AI programs meet enterprise risk standards before scaling up.

The number of AI regulations worldwide continues to increase. The EU AI Act establishes a risk-based oversight framework, with fines up to €35 million or 7% of the company's global turnover for the most serious violations. GDPR remains a powerful enforcement backdrop, with potential fines of up to €20 million or 4% of the company's global turnover. California has added legislative momentum to its governance with SB 53, a law that requires standardized safety disclosures for frontier AI developers, including incident reporting and whistleblower protections.

Companies also report that governance maturity is uneven. Recent research highlights that many senior data and AI leaders view their data and AI governance as insufficient; yet, they identify unified governance as a key enabler for moving from AI pilots to enterprise value. Harvard Business Review also observes that organizations that treat governance as an afterthought often struggle to scale AI pilots effectively. The practical takeaway here is that if an organization's governance is unclear, its risk is high, and its execution is slow.

This chapter gives executives a practical, testable framework to govern AI agents with confidence. Guidance is organized into three pillars: Safety Guardrails, Brand and Compliance, and Quality Control. Pillars are mapped to leading governance standards, so your program is auditable and scalable. We close with real implementation patterns and a roadmap that keeps innovation flowing while your risk profile stays within appetite.

Safety Guardrails

Guardrails are automated controls that reduce the probability and severity of incidents. A highway barrier is an appropriate analogy. You still need a skilled driver driving at a safe speed, but the barrier prevents catastrophic outcomes in the event of an accident

The risk landscape spans four layers:

1. **User-level risks**: toxic or biased content, hallucinations, or harmful recommendations
2. **Business risks**: off-brand or competitively sensitive disclosures
3. **Security risks**: prompt injection, jailbreaks, data exfiltration, and supply-chain abuse via tools and plug-ins
4. **Operational risks**: incorrect execution in critical systems, from payments to clinical workflows

Security researchers have identified and cataloged risks for LLM applications. The OWASP Top 10 for LLMs identifies prompt injection, data leaks, supply-chain weaknesses, and over-permissive tools as common failure modes. These need to be treated as the baseline checklist for red-team design and secure AI development.

Executives should recognize that guardrails are not a single product; instead, they are a set of tools and frameworks that include content filters, authorization boundaries, procedures, logging, and incident playbooks. NIST's AI Risk Management Framework emphasizes that governance is a continuous loop of Governance, Mapping, Measurement, and Management.

Technical Guardrail Implementation

Governance must show where an agent is constrained. The simplest way is to separate controls into input, output, and processing guardrails.

Input guardrails control what the agent can receive.

- **Toxicity and policy filters** prevent the model from ingesting hate, harassment, or illegal content that triggers unsafe response patterns later.
- **Jailbreak detection** searches for phrases and patterns designed to override system instructions.
- **Prompt-injection defense** treats any untrusted content as potentially adversarial, including user uploads and third-party knowledge bases.

- **Reference frameworks,** such as OWASP, identify specific attack patterns and tests to validate your coverage.

Output guardrails control what the agent can say or do.

- **Content safety filters** block high-risk outputs such as biased statements or unlicensed medical and legal advice.
- **Fact-checking and confidence thresholds** require citations, retrieval of evidence, or human review when confidence is low.
- **Topic management** keeps conversations within approved domains. Open-source and commercial solutions, including NVIDIA NeMo Guardrails, offer policy templates for defining topic boundaries and controlling tool access.
- **Action validation** requires verification before any high-stakes operation executes, such as fund transfers or record deletions.

Processing guardrails define how the agent operates.

- **Rate limiting** prevents runaway costs and denial-of-service patterns.
- **Least-privilege access** isolates the agent. Give only the permissions it needs.
- **Memory hygiene** enforces a time-to-live (TTL) on stored data, preventing the uncontrolled accumulation of personal or sensitive information.
- **Audit trails** create **immutable logs** of inputs, intermediate steps, tools invoked, and outputs.

Performance matters. In independent evaluations published by Cisco's Webex team, a production guardrail system achieved over 90% precision (not flagging normal content), recall (catching bad content), and F1 (tradeoff between precision and recall) against a hate-speech benchmark. Treat such figures as directional and validate with your own data and risk thresholds. The point is clear. Modern guardrails can be both effective and measurable.

Human-in-the-Loop Workflows

Automated guardrails reduce noise. Humans close the loop. Design risk-adaptive approval gates so that low-risk actions auto-execute, and higher-risk actions require sign-off.

Use a crisp matrix.

- **Require approval** for financial transactions above a defined threshold, any outbound communication to the C-suite or board, policy changes or exceptions, customer-facing communications during a live incident, and any action touching PII or protected data.

- **Support both synchronous approvals** for blocking steps and asynchronous reviews for batched proposals.
- **Define escalation paths** when reviewers disagree with the agent's recommendation.

Track the quality of the HITL review loop—agent proposes → reviewer approves / edits / declines → outcome logged and used to tune thresholds. Monitor false positives that cause unnecessary escalations and false negatives that miss real risk. Add time-to-approval to show operational friction and override frequency to learn where guardrails are too tight or too loose.

Fail-Safe Mechanisms and Incident Response

Incidents will happen. So, build the ability to pause, roll back, and recover from them.

- **Circuit breakers** trigger an automatic pause when error rates spike, complaint volumes surge, or external threat intelligence flags active attacks.
- **Rollback procedures** mirror modern software operations. Keep version control for prompts, retrieval rules, and model settings. Use blue-green deployments and be able to revert to the last known good state in minutes.
- **Incident classification** gives operations clarity.
    - **P0** for any data exposure, regulatory breach, or safety incident.
    - **P1** for brand damage, widespread errors, or suspected compliance issues.
    - **P2** for contained errors that still require follow-up.
    - **P3** for minor issues that you track for trend analysis.

Regulatory reporting timelines matter. GDPR's 72-hour breach notification clock starts when you become aware of a notifiable incident. Your playbook should reflect this timing and the EU AI Act's requirements for transparency and oversight when transacting using AI in the EU.

Brand Voice and Compliance

Agents interact at scale and at speed. If voice and tone shift by channel or by language, customers lose trust. Rigorous research on customer experience reveals a strong correlation with top-line revenue growth. McKinsey analysis finds CX leaders achieve more than double the revenue growth of laggards, and consistent, high-quality experiences are the differentiator. Agents are a visible part of that experience.

Customers also care about transparency. According to Salesforce's recent State of the AI Connected Customer report, 42% of customers stated that they trust businesses to use AI ethically, and 72% said it is important to know when they are communicating with an AI agent. Agents must disclose themselves and behave consistently with the brand promise.

Defining and Implementing Brand Voice for Agents

Document brand voice like you would a style guide for a newsroom.

- **Voice attributes** define whether you are friendly, formal, or technical.
- **Vocabulary** lists terms to use and terms to avoid.
- **Structural patterns** set expectations for sentence length, when to ask clarifying questions, and when to present options.
- **Cultural and regional guidance** addresses localization, holidays, and regulatory sensitivities.

Train agents with gold-standard examples from approved communications. Write custom instructions that express the brand voice and the legal limits of what the agent can say. Run A/B tests against human-written responses and measure consistency scores over time. Commercial platforms can be helpful, but the core discipline lies in your own content library and review cycle.

Legal and Regulatory Compliance

Compliance does not need to slow down an organization. It must be designed from day one. Map the company's compliance obligations into a compliance implementation checklist.

- **Data governance**: storage location, access rights, and retention policies.
- **Consent and disclosure**: clear user notice when an AI agent is in use and a path to opt out.
- **Explainability**: an auditable reason for each high-stakes decision.
- **Audit trail**: immutable, query-able logs of inputs, processing steps, and actions.
- **Right to contest**: a clear process and an actual human reviewer.

- **Oversight**: documented human review for high-risk actions and periodic audits.

Use recognized frameworks to accelerate alignment. NIST's AI RMF structures risk management activities. ISO/IEC 42001 defines an AI management system that formalizes oversight, logging, and continual improvement. Together, they provide the scaffolding to show boards and regulators that your controls are systematic, repeatable, and improvable.

California's SB 53 signals a broader direction in the United States. It establishes standardized disclosure requirements for frontier model developers and provides protections for whistleblowers. Even if you do not develop models, your vendors may do so, and your contracts should reflect these obligations.

Quality Control and Continuous Improvement

Agents are software, and therefore, they must be treated with the same observability rigor expected for any production system.

Performance metrics should include task completion rate, time to resolution, escalation rate, and user satisfaction.

Quality metrics should track observed accuracy, adherence to brand voice, hallucination rates, and safety trigger rates from your guardrails.

Business metrics should be tied to cost per interaction, deflection rates, and revenue impact, where applicable.

Log everything you need to reconstruct a decision. Use structured logs and trace IDs to follow multi-agent workflows. Protect privacy by excluding PII from logs and applying role-based access controls to telemetry.

Testing and Validation Strategies

Build a test culture that reflects your risk appetite.

- **Red team testing** fires adversarial prompts drawn from the OWASP LLM Top 10 against your system and tools. Run this after any significant change and at least quarterly for high-risk use cases.
- **Continuous testing** maintains a synthetic test set of known good and known bad inputs. Every deployment runs a regression suite, and new versions can run in **shadow mode** before a full cutover.
- **Canary releases** roll out to a small share of users and monitors leading indicators before broader exposure.

- **A/B testing** compares prompt strategies, model versions, and guardrail thresholds. Prioritize user satisfaction and task success first, and evaluate the cost alongside them.

Feedback Loops and Iteration

Close the loop with in-conversation ratings, issue flags, and post-interaction surveys. Pair this with internal QA audits that sample transcripts and score them for accuracy, tone, and policy compliance.

Maintain an edge-case library so unusual scenarios become training data. Hold a weekly metrics review to triage urgent fixes, a monthly deep-dive to plan experiments, and a quarterly red-team and guardrail recalibration.

Avoid common pitfalls.

- Do not over-optimize a single metric at the expense of accuracy or trust.
- Do not ignore long-tail issues. At scale, they add up.
- Do not mistake dashboards for outcomes. Pair quantitative metrics with qualitative review.

Building a Governance Framework That Scales

Beyond guardrails, strong governance is about embedding accountability, repeatability, and resilience into the way in which AI agents are deployed and utilized. Without clear roles and a roadmap, even the best controls remain fragmented and ineffective. Executives should treat governance as a business operating model, considering *who makes decisions, how they are made, and how maturity evolves.*

The simplest way to institutionalize AI governance is through the establishment of an AI Governance Council. Set up the council, chaired by a C-level executive and leaders from legal, risk, security, data, and the operating units that deploy agents. Meet monthly for regular reviews, quarterly for deep dives, and on an ad-hoc basis for incidents. The governance council sets principles and risk appetite, approves high-risk use cases, and allocates budget for governance tools and training.

Day-to-day, three roles matter most:

1. **AI Governance Lead**: Owns the framework and coordinates audits and incident management.

2. **AI Security Specialist**: Threat modeling, penetration testing, and supply-chain review.
3. **AI Ethics Specialist**: Bias evaluation, fairness reviews, and societal impact assessment.

Organizations typically progress through five stages of maturity:

1. **Ad-hoc**: heroics and reactivity.
2. **Documented**: policies exist, compliance is partial.
3. **Standardized**: enterprise standards, regular audits.
4. **Managed**: measurable outcomes, continuous improvement.
5. **Optimizing**: predictive, benchmarked, and externally recognized.

Aligning With Industry Frameworks

Instead of attempting to reinvent the wheel, utilize recognized frameworks to shorten the governance process development and simplify audits.

- **NIST AI RMF**: Organize activities into Governance, Map, Measurement, and Management. This provides you with a common language for risk and compliance teams to communicate effectively.
- **ISO/IEC 42001**: Implement an AI management system that formalizes oversight, logging, supplier controls, and improvement cycles. Helpful for global operations and international certification.
- **COBIT**: Integrate AI governance into broader IT governance. COBIT's 40 governance and management objectives across EDM, APO, BAI, DSS, and MEA align cleanly with enterprise control catalogs. ISACA's recent guidance shows how to apply COBIT to AI systems.

Governance in the Real-World and Implementation Examples

Designing HIPAA-Compliant AI Architectures

Healthcare leaders want to deploy AI agents for patient scheduling, billing, and inquiry management. But they want to do so without violating HIPAA requirements for privacy, auditability, and secure data handling.

Academic researchers have proposed agentic AI designs that explicitly align with the safeguards outlined in HIPAA. A 2025 study outlines an architecture featuring attribute-based access control, hybrid sanitization, and immutable audit trails, ensuring the protection of PHI while still facilitating helpful patient interactions. Complementary analyses stress that ethical AI in clinical practice must integrate regulatory guardrails, explainability, and continuous oversight.

These implementations are currently in an academic setting or remain in the early stages. Yet they illustrate how governance frameworks (privacy controls, oversight bodies, and explainability standards) can make hospitals more confident in testing and learning with AI without exceeding regulatory boundaries.

Bank of America's Erica Virtual Assistant

Banks must innovate in client experience while meeting strict regulations on data privacy, audit, and compliance. Any AI system handling sensitive financial data must log every interaction, align with supervisory rules, and protect customer trust.

Bank of America launched **Erica**, its AI-powered financial assistant, in 2018 with governance embedded into its architecture. Interactions get logged for compliance, functionality is tightly scoped to advisory guidelines, and escalation to humans is required for regulated advice. Internal rollouts also included employee-facing agents, reducing IT service desk load by more than 50%.

By 2025, Erica had surpassed 3 billion interactions with over 50 million clients, making it one of the most scaled AI deployments in financial services. CIO Dive notes Erica's launch strategy as an example of careful scaling with a measurable ROI. Erica demonstrates how compliance-aligned governance unlocks adoption even in highly regulated sectors.

E-Commerce: Scaling Brand Voice with AI Content Systems

Global e-commerce companies often struggle to maintain a consistent brand voice across thousands of product listings, blogs, and marketing campaigns. Without governance, AI risks producing inconsistent tone or non-compliant messaging.

One e-commerce platform documented by Shelly Palmer deployed AI systems to automate product descriptions and content creation at scale. To preserve brand identity, they trained models on approved style guides and paired automation with editorial review loops.

The company achieved a 113% increase in blog output, a 7% uplift in site traffic, and freed human editors to focus on higher-value strategic work. These results align with broader research indicating that a consistent brand presentation can drive 23–33% higher revenue. The case illustrates that governance of tone, vocabulary, and approvals is crucial for scale AI without diluting the brand.

Conclusion: Governance as Competitive Advantage

The narrative that governance slows innovation is outdated. The top performers capitalizing on AI combine ambitious AI roadmaps with visible, consistent governance. They release faster because teams are familiar with the rules. They scale with confidence because incidents are rare, and when they occur, the response is fast and disciplined. CEO-level oversight of AI governance is correlated with a higher EBIT impact. Treat governance as a leadership responsibility, not a back-office function.

There is a simple financial calculus —budget 10 to 15% of your AI program for governance, operations, and controls. Skimping on that investment is usually more expensive. A single breach can cost millions. Regulatory violations can add up to eight-figure penalties, but brand damage often lasts far longer than any fine.

Build trust through transparency. Tell users when they are engaging an agent. Offer a path to contest decisions. Explain how the system works at a level that a reasonable customer can understand. Make governance visible. Publish your principles. Show your audit trail maturity to boards, customers, and partners. Keep learning. AI capabilities and risks evolve. Your governance must evolve with them.

Three near-term actions for executives

1. **Stand up an AI Governance Council this quarter.** Assign roles. Set principles. Inventory risks.
2. **Implement basic guardrails before scale.** Control inputs, outputs, and high-stakes actions. Enable logging and create an incident playbook.
3. **Treat compliance as a product requirement.** Map to NIST and ISO 42001 now. Prepare for EU AI Act obligations and emerging state laws such as California's SB 53.

Looking forward, the regulatory trajectory is clear—the EU AI Act phases in across 2024 to 2030. Multiple states in the U.S. are stepping up with targeted rules. Early movers that hard-wire governance into product and operating rhythms will grow faster and spend less time firefighting.

References:

- What is the EU AI Act? | IBM
- Transparency in Frontier Artificial Intelligence Act (SB-53): California Requires New Standardized AI Safety Disclosures
- New Economist Impact Study Finds Only 22% of Enterprises Believe Their IT Infrastructure is Ready for AI - Databricks
- What Companies with Successful AI Pilots Do Differently
- OWASP Top 10 for LLM Applications 2025
- AI Risk Management Framework | NIST
- AI Guardrails: Content Moderation and Safety with Open Language Models | Haystack
- AI Guardrails: Ensuring Safe and Reliable Language Model Deployment
- Art. 33 GDPR – Notification of a personal data breach to the supervisory authority - General Data Protection Regulation (GDPR)
- Experience-led growth: A new way to create value
- Salesforce's State of the Connected Customer report
- Artificial Intelligence Risk Management Framework (AI RMF 1.0) | NIST
- ISO/IEC 42001: a new standard for AI governance
- California's Newsom signs law requiring AI safety disclosures | Reuters
- ISACA Now Blog 2025 AI Governance and the Need for Auditors Well Trained in AI
- [2504.17669] Towards a HIPAA Compliant Agentic AI System in Healthcare
- Ethical and regulatory challenges of AI technologies in healthcare: A narrative review - PMC
- AI Adoption by BofA's Global Workforce Improves Productivity, Client Service | Press Releases | Newsroom | Bank of America
- A Decade of AI Innovation: BofA's Virtual Assistant Erica Surpasses 3 Billion Client Interactions | Press Releases | Newsroom
- Case Study: Scaling Content Creation with AI for an E-commerce Platform | Shelly Palmer
- 40 Brand Voice Consistency Statistics in eCommerce in 2025
- The state of AI: How organizations are rewiring to capture value

CHAPTER 10

Measuring Success – ROI that matters to the Board

Boards are increasing AI budgets while simultaneously complaining about thin or invisible returns. That is the paradox you must resolve.

Most large organizations claim that AI is now in production somewhere. McKinsey research reports that 78% of them use AI in at least one function, yet many have not translated activity into bottom-line impact.

Google Cloud's latest enterprise study reports that 74% of executives achieve ROI within the first year, and 52% say their organizations have deployed AI agents. At the same time, sober analyses show the gap between AI spending and value.

IBM's 2025 CEO Study reports that over the past three years, only 25% of AI initiatives delivered an expected ROI, and only 16% of organizations have scaled enterprise-wide.

IDC research likewise highlights scale-up as a significant business problem: 88% of AI pilots/POCs fail to reach production. Most organizations report skill, governance, and data hurdles that stall the value that could be captured from AI.

What explains the contradiction? It is down to measurement.

Traditional IT performance metrics track delivery and cost. Agentic AI creates value in several places at once: time back for teams, happier customers who stay, fewer errors and risks, and faster testing of ideas. If we measure only one dimension, say labor savings in one team, we undercount the return. Yet the upside is real. IDC estimates that every new $1 spent on AI solutions could add about $4.60 to the global economy by 2030.

Setting Your Organization Up to Win

Why AI programs stall

Failure patterns repeat. Data quality is the first limiter of any successful AI program. Eighty-five percent of organizations cite data quality as the biggest challenge in their AI strategies. Without clean, accessible volumes of data, agents cannot resolve full workflows or make correct writebacks. Ownership and coordination are the second limiter. Additionally, IDC and others have found that many AI initiatives lack clear executive sponsorship and cross-functional alignment.

ROI expectations are often unclear at the outset, which undermines prioritization and post-implementation credibility. In one recent enterprise survey, 36% of organizations cited a lack of well-defined ROI expectations as a mistake they made in past AI initiatives.

Other common brakes include talent gaps and regulatory/compliance hurdles, especially in regulated sectors.

Minimum viable data and integration

Before forecasting ROI, put in a minimum viable data stack. Establish a simple, auditable data governance schema. Document data lineage for key data sources that agents will use to read and write. Instrument quality checks for freshness, completeness, and field-level accuracy. Provide API access to systems of record, allowing agents to close the loop by reading a record, taking an action, and writing the outcome back to the source of truth. Teams that skip this fundamental groundwork rarely reach scale production.

Gartner forecasts that at least 30% of GenAI projects will be abandoned after PoC by the end of 2025, while S&P Global/451 Research reports a 46% median abandonment rate pre-production, with data/integration and unclear value among the top causes.

Three-tier readiness assessment

Timelines and ROI for AI agents vary depending on organizational readiness. Typical delivery windows for well-run AI projects are 3–6 months from pilot to production, with some projects taking up to a year for more extensive integration. High ROI outliers exist in specific, well-scoped deployments. Treat company size thresholds guidelines, not gatekeepers.

Readiness = data + integration + sponsorship.

This is a fast triage for business planning, not a maturity score. Use it to scope investment and timelines. It helps to decide what to tackle first, how long it will take, and the likely investment-to-return ratio based on three key ingredients: data foundation, integration pathways, and executive sponsorship. Ranges are indicative, not promises; regulated contexts or heavy tech debt trend longer/higher.

Rule of thumb: if you match two of the three ingredients for a tier, plan with that tier. When in doubt, plan for the lower tier.

1. **Tier 1. High-readiness organizations.** Clean, accessible data. Executive sponsorship at the VP+ level. Prior automation wins. Cross-functional team in place. 4-week pilot and 12-week implementation are typical. Target outcome: 150–250% ROI in the first year from a well-scoped use case. Investment $75K–$250K. Often $50M+ revenue or 500+ employees.

2. **Tier 2. Medium-readiness.** Partial data readiness with gaps. Limited AI expertise but willingness to partner. A 2-month preparation period, followed by a pilot, and then a 16-week build. Target outcome: 100–200% ROI within 12 months. Investment $100K–$350K. $10M–$50M revenue or 100–500 employees.

3. **Tier 3. Foundation-building.** Scattered data, minimal prior automation, weak documentation, legacy constraints. Expect a 6-month foundation phase before the pilot. Target outcome: 50–150% first-year ROI once the first use case is in production and adoption stabilizes. Investment $150K–$500K including data plumbing. Often < $10M revenue or <100 employees, or larger firms with heavy tech debt.

Critical success factors to avoid "Pilot Purgatory" for any tier:

- Executive sponsorship with a committed budget.
- A supportive, single business owner with P&L accountability.
- Measurable current-state metrics and a clearly defined digital process.
- Confirmed data access of sufficient quality and quantity to proceed.
- Willingness to redesign workflows, not just overlay a digital assistant on broken workflows.

If any of the following are true, hit pause and fix foundations:

- There is no quantifiable business problem.
- Nobody can explain the current process costs or flow.
- Critical data exists, but only in spreadsheets or mailboxes.
- Prior IT projects routinely stall.
- Our leaders have unrealistic delivery expectations and demand a two-week implementation for a multi-system workflow that takes months to build, test, and implement.

Those flags correlate with the high abandonment rates we mentioned earlier.

The four-pillar ROI framework

Boards care about outcomes that hit the income statement and protect enterprise value. Utilize a four-pillar approach that encompasses tangible strategic returns.

Keep the math simple and conservative. Your CFO will add the complexity to the spreadsheet.

1. **Efficiency gains**. Time, labor, and process improvements.
2. **Revenue generation**. Conversion, retention, capacity to serve.
3. **Risk mitigation**. Compliance, security, and quality costs avoided.
4. **Business agility**. Speed, adaptation, and option value.

Pillar one: Efficiency gains

What to measure: Measure end-to-end workflows rather than isolated tasks. Track labor hours saved, fully loaded. Include cycle-time improvements and error-rate reductions. Count software licenses or infrastructure you can retire.

Benchmarks: Support agents using AI tools handle 13.8% more inquiries per hour. Controlled studies show knowledge workers are 33% more productive during hours when they use GenAI for suitable tasks. When scoped effectively, service operations typically achieve double-digit cost reductions.

Pillar two: Revenue generation

What to measure: Track conversion rates, lead quality, and sales cycle velocity. For subscription businesses, quantify churn reduction and upsell. Attribute conservatively. I recommend allocating 50–70% of the attribution to the agentic system when multiple initiatives run concurrently.

Benchmarks: Personalization at scale remains one of the most reliable levers for driving growth. McKinsey reports that companies successfully delivering personalization can expect a 10–15% revenue uplift. According to Salesforce, teams that use AI for sales prospecting and content generation can streamline campaign development and scale personalized engagement more efficiently.

Pillar three: Risk mitigation

What to measure?

Quantify avoided costs: fines, penalties, breach remediation, SLA penalties, fraud losses, and the rework costs of quality failures. Express each as a probability-weighted expectation.

The cost of failure here is not immaterial. We have already noted that the global average cost of a data breach is $4.45 million.

Pillar four: Business agility

What to measure: Decision speed. Experimentation velocity. Time to market. The number of initiatives the same team can support. Option value created by reusable capabilities.

Why it matters: AI leaders report 20–30% improvements in productivity, speed to market, and revenue from systematic deployment at scale. Google Cloud's 2025 study shows that firms investing in agentic capabilities are more likely to report a first-year ROI and to quickly expand to adjacent use cases.

How to discuss this with the board: Use a before-and-after narrative with time stamps and headcount. Example: "Product launches required six months with three marketers. After the agentic content-ops pipeline, launches require six weeks with two marketers, plus an agent that personalizes and tests copy across channels." Tie agility to share gain, quicker cash inflows, and optionality.

Building the Business Case

Your business case should fit on one page for the executive summary, backed by a spreadsheet that a finance partner can audit.

Executive summary (one page):
The problem: Quantify the status quo. For example, "Average response time is 4.2 hours and cost per interaction is $12.50."
The solution: Specific agentic capabilities tied to one workflow.
The investment: Year-by-year cost. One-time vs. recurring.
The return: Expected ROI across the four pillars with conservative assumptions.
The timeline: Milestones and payback period.
The risk: Cost of inaction and risk mitigation plan.

Investment breakdown (illustrative planning ranges)

Cost category	Year 1	Year 2	Year 3
One-time costs			
Discovery and design	$15–25K	–	–
Development and integration	$50–150K	–	–
Data infrastructure	$20–50K	–	Upgrades as needed
Training and change management	$15–30K	$5–10K	$5–10K
Recurring costs			
Platform and infrastructure	$24–60K	$24–60K	$24–60K
Model API costs	$12–36K	$12–36K	$12–36K
Maintenance and optimization	20% of dev	20% of dev	20% of dev
Total investment	**$136–351K**	**$41–106K**	**$41–106K**

These ranges align with current market evidence on pilot-to-platform efforts and reflect the 3–6 month implementation windows seen in industry programs.

Scenario modeling. Present three scenarios with explicit probabilities.

- **Conservative (60%):** Efficiency +15%; churn reduction 5%. **Year 1 ROI: 85–120%**. Payback in **8–11 months**.
- **Moderate (30%):** Efficiency +25%; churn reduction 15% plus 5% upsell. **Year 1 ROI: 150–200%**. Payback **5–7 months**.
- **Aggressive (10%):** Efficiency +35% or more; churn reduction 25% plus 10% upsell. **Year 1 ROI: 250–333%**. Payback **3–4 months**.

Document every assumption: volumes, rates, attribution share, and loaded costs. For sensitivity analysis, vary adoption, volume, and deflection by ±10 points to identify break-points that matter to finance.

Metrics dashboard and tracking

Pre-implementation baseline: Treat baseline data as your "before photo." Collect at least **three months** of pre-implementation metrics. Six to twelve months is better for smoothing seasonality. Capture median and p90 for response and resolution times, CSAT or NPS, agent productivity, escalation rate, cost per interaction, and error or rework rates.

Implementation tracking (weekly): Uptime and availability. Agent accuracy and human escalation rates. Adoption. Spend vs. budget.

Ongoing performance dashboard (monthly):

Metric	Baseline	Current	Target	Trend
Avg response time	4.2 hours	1.8 hours	<2.0 hours	↓ 57%
CSAT	3.8/5.0	4.3/5.0	>4.2	↑ 13%
Cost per interaction	$12.50	$8.75	<$9.00	↓ 30%
Churn rate	12% annual	9.5% annual	<10%	↓ 21%

Quarterly board summary: Present a single, cohesive view of progress and impact: how many interactions the AI system handled versus human teams, the revenue retained or generated with supporting methodology, costs avoided with documented assumptions, and the cumulative ROI to date. Close with a brief review of key risks, mitigations, and next-phase recommendations to keep oversight focused on outcomes rather than activity.

Company-size-specific guidance

SMB ($1M–$10M revenue, <100 employees): Focus on quick wins in customer support triage and lead qualification. Plan $25K–$75K for a pilot and $75K–$150K to scale. Expect positive ROI in 6–12 months. Choose turnkey tools and avoid heavy custom builds.

Mid-market ($10M–$100M revenue, 100–1,000 employees): Target department-level transformation: customer success swarms, sales enablement, or marketing automation. Plan $100K–$350K for a comprehensive solution. ROI often turns positive within 3–9 months if you have clean data and exec sponsorship.

Enterprise ($100M+ revenue, 1,000+ employees): Pursue platform plays across multiple functions. Budget $250K–$1M+ for an enterprise capability with shared APIs, identity, and observability. ROI is typically 6–18 months but scales to a very large absolute value. Build an internal center of excellence to standardize patterns and avoid one-off rebuilds. These ranges reflect current enterprise patterns and the platform investments described in scale-up case work.

Real-world ROI examples

Customer service transformation

In 2025, Verizon reported a nearly 40% sales increase, attributed to an AI assistant that supports 28,000 service representatives with faster answers from 15,000 internal documents. The system reduced call times and unlocked more time for value-added sales conversations.

Sales enablement

Lumen Technologies' sales teams utilized Microsoft Copilot to compress seller research from four hours to fifteen minutes, resulting in a projected $50M in annual time-savings value. The program combined Copilot with connectors to enterprise data, allowing the agent to summarize interactions, harvest insights, and propose next steps within the seller workflow.

Marketing automation

A recent Forrester TEI study of an agentic platform found a 333% ROI and $12.02M NPV over three years, with under six-month payback, 85% reduction in review times, and 65% faster onboarding for the composite enterprise studied.

Common ROI Pitfalls to Avoid

Vanity metrics: "Agent answered 10,000 queries" is not a result. "Agent resolved 35% of tier-1 inquiries with 4.2/5 CSAT, saving 280 hours weekly" is a result. Boards fund outcomes, not volume of AI activity. Report throughput only insofar as it drives outcomes, such as resolution rate, cycle time, unit cost, revenue, or risk. Tie each metric back to the four pillars (efficiency, revenue, risk, and agility) so finance can book the impact.

No baseline: If you do not capture pre-implementation performance for 3–6 months, you cannot prove a delta. Treat baseline capture as phase zero.

Attribution errors: Overclaiming AI results when multiple initiatives drive the same KPIs can undermine credibility. Attribute 50–70% (this figure really depends on the project specifics) of the ROI impact to AI when multiple initiatives contribute and document your method.

Ignoring hidden costs: Software is not the total cost. Budget 20–30% for change management and 20% annually for ongoing optimization. These are common ranges in enterprise programs and are frequently underestimated in early plans. Also, call out common omissions, including security review, procurement cycles, data labeling, model risk management (for regulated entities), and integration hardening.

Short-term thinking: AI agents learn and improve with use and time. Evaluate their performance over 12–24 months and show learning curves with 30/60/90-day checkpoints. Plot adoption, human-in-the-loop rate, resolution rate, and unit cost. Tie the trend line to the Ongoing performance dashboard cadence so improvements flow into the ROI roll-up.

Strategic missteps: Don't try to boil the ocean. Start with a narrow, high-pain business use case tied to a P&L owner. Technology follows strategy, not the reverse. Treat the program as a product with weekly optimization and monthly performance analysis. Build the governance, security, and integration rails early to avoid the "pilot traps".

Conclusion: From measurement to action

Make the mindset shift. AI agents should move you from a cost center to a profit center. With a scoped use case, clean data, and change management, a 6–12 months to payback is a reasonable target. Build once, expand across adjacencies. Pilots have value only when they lead to production at scale. That is where the four pillars show up on financial statements.

Three actions for immediate impact.

1. Run the three-tier readiness assessment. Close obvious gaps.
2. Build your business case. Gather baseline metrics now, even if the build doesn't start until next quarter. Model conservative, moderate, and aggressive scenarios and stress-test with finance.
3. Start with one high-pain, measurable workflow. Budget for integration and change management. Instrument from day one.

The companies that achieve 200–333% ROI have clear problem statements, invest in readiness, and measure rigorously. They also treat AI as a strategic transformation, not a tooling project. The companies that join the failure statistics follow a script, too. They skip the basics, underestimate data and integration, ignore change management, and expect magic results instead of redesigning their processes to achieve optimal business outcomes. The choice is yours.

References:

- Ballooning AI budgets expected to face ROI pressure
- ROI remains elusive for enterprise AI plans despite progress
- The state of AI: How organizations are rewiring to capture value
- Google Cloud Study Reveals 52% of Executives Say Their Organizations Have Deployed AI Agents, Unlocking a New Wave of Business Value
- IBM Study: CEOs Double Down on AI While Navigating Enterprise Hurdles
- 88% of AI pilots fail to reach production — but that's not all on IT | CIO
- IDC: Artificial Intelligence Will Contribute $19.9 Trillion to the Global Economy through 2030 and Drive 3.5% of Global GDP in 2030
- KPMG AI Quarterly Pulse Survey
- The Next Generation of AI: More than Half of Companies (51%) Already Deployed AI Agents
- Gartner Predicts 30% of Generative AI Projects Will Be Abandoned After Proof of Concept By End of 2025
- 451 IT Insider: A roundup for IT decision-makers (June) | S&P Global
- The Complexities of Measuring AI ROI | Devoteam
- The Total Economic Impact™ Of Writer | Forrester
- AI Tools Raise the Productivity of Customer-Support Agents - NN/G
- The Impact of Generative AI on Work Productivity | St. Louis Fed
- The value of getting personalization right—or wrong—is multiplying | McKinsey
- Harnessing AI for Sales Prospecting | Salesforce
- Cost of a Data Breach Report 2025
- 2025 AI Business Predictions: PwC
- How agents are unlocking the next wave of AI-driven business value.
- Verizon says Google AI for customer service agents has led to sales jump | Reuters
- Lumen's strategic leap: How Copilot is redefining productivity and employee engagement | Microsoft Customer Stories
- Key Findings from the Forrester Total Economic Impact™ study on WRITER

CHAPTER 11

The Build vs. Buy Decision Framework

Over 80% of AI projects fail, which is roughly twice the failure rate of traditional IT projects. That is not internet folklore. It's a sobering finding echoed in a 2024 study from the RAND Corporation, which analyzed the "anti-patterns" that derail AI initiatives. In 2025, S&P Global reported a sharp reversal in AI momentum: the share of companies that abandoned most of their AI initiatives jumped from 17% to 42% in a single year.

Gartner's independent forecast aligns with this direction: at least 30% of GenAI projects will be abandoned after proof-of-concept by the end of 2025 - largely due to poor data, weak risk controls, and unclear business value. And MIT's Project NANDA adds a more stinging coda: only about 5% of generative-AI pilots deliver rapid revenue acceleration; the rest stall with little measurable P&L impact whatsoever.

That is the backdrop for your build-vs-buy decision on agentic AI. You're not choosing between two tech strategies; you're selecting a path with explicit consequences for time-to-value, cost, risk, competitive advantage, and most critically, your probability of shipping an AI solution or strategy that has an achievable and measurable business impact.

In today's market, almost every company is investing in AI, yet just 1% say they have reached AI maturity. This chapter provides a candid view of AI to help you decide what to build, what to buy, and when a hybrid build-and-buy approach is a winning move.

Understanding the High Stakes

Traditional software is like following a recipe. If you use the same ingredients and steps, you'll always get the same result. That's called deterministic AI.

Agentic AI is probabilistic. Results change with data, context, and feedback. Early architectural choices therefore echo for years through integration, operating cost, and compliance. The wrong early decision amplifies later risks, e.g., fragile integrations, hidden operating costs, and compliance gaps that only surface at scale. This chapter addresses this choice: build in-house or buy with a partner.

While McKinsey highlights large productivity potential from AI, and reports that organizations are beginning to take steps that drive bottom-line impact by redesigning workflows, only 1% of organizations say they have achieved AI maturity. A related reality is that a significant portion of lifecycle costs accrues post-deployment, including maintenance, integration, hardening, monitoring, and governance. Early architectural choices compound in impact, both positive and negative, over the years, and utilize AI solutions.

The AI DIY Reality Check

Internal builds often fail for predictable reasons. Most problems can be traced back to brittle data, weak application integration, poorly defined goals, or a lack of governance. To fix this, we must understand each fail pattern, why it blocks production-winning code, and fix it for that. The goal here is not to argue against building an application. It is to give you a clear risk map and checklist to manage against, if you choose the DIY path, so that you don't fail.

Common Failure Patterns in Internal AI Development

Data quality traps: Machine learning systems do not "figure it out" later; they encode your current data reality. RAND's research report highlights data limitations as a primary driver of AI program failure. Why? Data leakage, biased data samples, or insufficient volume of quality data are the repeated sources of AI program failure. Enterprises systematically underestimate the effort required to clean, tag, govern, and serve data to AI agents reliably, without latency.

Integration nightmares: Organizations must not treat the ML code as the entire AI ecosystem. An AI ecosystem encompasses data pipelines, retrieval layers, user access, identity, and permissions, as well as a messaging bus and a change-management cadence. Governance afterthoughts**:** Teams that bolt on compliance late in the project life cycle get burnt. Effective AI programs implement risk controls, logging, and human-in-the-loop checkpoints from day zero. We argued this in Chapter 9, and in that chapter, when AI program guardrails were mapped to NIST and ISO standards for auditability.

The Talent Gap Challenge

Talent is the choke point in AI. Scarcity and skill gaps slow teams more than tools or models. Most failures trace back to missing people, limited experience, and slow hiring. Scarcity raises costs. Conventional developers struggle with agents. Wage premiums push the total cost of ownership higher.

The scarcity of expertise: Investment in AI has outpaced the labor market's ability to supply experienced talent. Bain projects a U.S. AI hiring gap of approximately 50% with demand for skilled AI talent potentially exceeding the talent supply by 700,000 workers over the next two years. Bain further reports that 44% of executives cite a lack of in-house AI expertise as a primary barrier to the implementation of GenAI. Randstad's 2024 global survey likewise shows a steep rise in job postings requiring AI skills and persistent scarcity across markets.

Traditional software developers may struggle to understand and implement AI agents, as agentic systems differ from conventional apps. They are probabilistic, depend on retrieval strategies and prompt orchestration, and require human-in-the-loop patterns that most teams have never shipped.

These gaps show up in maturity data. McKinsey notes that organizations **invest broadly in AI while remaining early in maturity**. Capabilities and operating models lag ambition. Without specialists in prompt design, retrieval, and evaluation, and safety and monitoring, teams stack up proofs of concept and stall before production.

The cost of competing for talent: Wages for AI-skilled roles have moved faster than general tech compensation. Employers currently pay distinct premiums for AI skills. For example, Oxford Internet Institute's 2025 analysis shows AI skills carry a 23% average wage premium across roles (and a higher differential in science/engineering), outpacing many other degree premiums. Even if you hire AI generalists, upskilling costs and time-to-competence are non-trivial, and your freshly trained team is immediately on competitors' recruiting radar. IBM highlights a widening training gap, a 50% talent shortfall (needed skills include GenAI and LLM basics, prompt-tuning), and the need for security and privacy skills plus C-suite literacy.

Real DIY Costs and Timelines

Budgets fail when leaders price only the model and ignore the system. Real cost sits in data plumbing, integration, security, and ongoing operations. This section outlines likely ranges for spending and timeline, and makes plausible estimates based on the cited sources. It flags hidden line items that trigger overruns and explains why underestimating testing adds months. Use it to sketch a credible three-year TCO and to choose a fast path to production.

Financial reality: Published market ranges for custom enterprise AI builds are consistently six-figure to low seven-figure when accounting for integration, data work, and security: $100,000–$500,000+ for enterprise-grade implementations is common corridor; more ambitious, cross-system builds can cost between $2,500,000–$4,800,000 all-in. Hidden costs include building the data plumbing, model monitoring, compliance reviews, the cost of creating incident playbooks, and code re-work as requirements evolve. Organizations that run under budget and disregard these costs are more likely to fail.

Timeline reality: Professional implementations typically reach production in 4–6 months; DIY software builds can take between 12–18 months before a stable production environment is created, if it even gets there. When companies say an agent application will take between "10–12 weeks" to go live, they are usually describing a minimum timeline for a targeted deployment with a very controlled scope; credible guides recommend allocating around 30% of that time to testing. We have already observed that nearly half of POCs are scrapped before production. Yet, every month you delay, a competitor can lock in channel advantages and data feedback loops ahead of you.

Risk factors: The statistical picture converges: 30–50% of initiatives never make it past the prototype stage, and 42% of firms scrapped most of their AI efforts in 2025 (Gartner summary; S&P Global via *CIO Dive*). Scope creep, knowledge loss from attrition, and governance retrofits are the usual suspects.

When Building in-house makes sense

There **are** legitimate reasons for your internal team to build agentic AI systems:

- **AI is a core differentiator:** If your competitive moats hinge on proprietary data and workflow nuance, off-the-shelf, one-size-fits-all templated AI products won't fit.
- **You already have a seasoned team:** Real ML engineers, data scientists, and architects with production credits.
- **You have time and budget:** 12–18 months to learn, iterate, and harden; a tolerance for several failed experiments along the way.
- **Your requirements are truly unique:** Market tools don't address your constraints or controls.

For everyone else, choose the hybrid path. Buy a proven base to deliver value now. Build internal capability in parallel. (For planning ROI and proving value early, use the measurement approach in Chapter 10.)

The Professional Implementation Advantage

Professional implementation changes the odds. Experienced teams arrive with established patterns, controls, and the necessary skills on day one. They shorten the path to production, reduce rework, and surface risks early. The goal is not outsourcing for its own sake. It is a faster value, clearer costs, and a system your team can operate and extend.

Battle-tested architecture

Experienced partners have *seen your movie before*. They bring patterns, accelerators, governance templates, and program experience refined across dozens of deployments. They also know where projects can crack apart—data contracts, identity boundaries, and evaluation harnesses—and engineer those from day one.

Speed to value

Reaching first production for a scoped agentic AI use case typically takes 4–6 months with an experienced partner. DIY efforts often need 12–18 months. Partners arrive with cross-functional teams across data engineering, machine learning, application integration, security, and QA. This avoids a hiring ramp for these skills. Work runs in parallel on data, integration, and safety, which shortens the critical path to production. Faster cycles create faster feedback loops, so you start collecting real user, cost, and quality signals while competitors are still in the staffing phase.

Risk mitigation

Vendors amortize AI R&D across many clients and ship with established governance. Professional teams front-load risk identification, testing, and observability, which increases the likelihood that your pilot will reach production. And because the scope and deliverables are clearer, the cost variance narrows compared with DIY teams discovering complexity mid-build.

A practical TCO comparison

Over a three-year horizon, a DIY program commonly includes:

Year 1

- **Hiring a core team** (e.g., senior ML engineer, data engineer, backend/integration engineer, product/QA): $300K–$500K total cash comp
- **Data and infrastructure setup:** $100K
- **Application development:** $200K–$400K
- **Experiments and rework contingency:** $100K–$200K (often needed and often underfunded)

Years 2–3 (per year)

- **Team salaries** for the internal build team noted above: $300K–$500K
- **Maintenance and monitoring:** $100K
- **Tools and platform licenses:** $50K
- **Training and upskilling:** $50K

  Total (3 years): $1.5M–$2.5M

  Time to production: 12–18 months

Success probability: roughly one-third.

Third-party implementation path (typical 3-year view):

This means hiring a professional third-party implementation partner and running on a commercial platform. The aim is faster time to value, lower execution risk, and structured knowledge transfer to your team.

Year 1

- **Partner services** for discovery, solution design, data work, integration, security, QA, and knowledge transfer: $150K–$300K
- **Platform subscription:** $60K
- **Targeted customization and integration:** $50K–$100K

Years 2–3 (per year)

- **Platform subscription:** $60K
- **Partner support and maintenance:** $30K
- **Internal training / Centre of Excellence:** $20K

  Total (3 years): $500K–$800K

  Time to production: 4–6 months

Success rates are closer to two-thirds, according to MIT, which reports that purchased solutions paired with the right partners dramatically outperform in-house builds in terms of time-to-impact.

These are planning ranges, not guarantees, but they reflect what the 2024–2025 body of evidence says about time, risk, and cost drivers. Actuals vary depending on the scope, security requirements, and usage volumes. (See the ROI model scaffolding in Chapter 10 for how to present this to boards.)

A Decision Framework for Executives to Use

The five assessment dimensions

1) Core competency analysis

Is AI **central** to your differentiation? Do you possess proprietary data or workflows that a market product cannot capture? Will your agentic AI capability define your market position?

Decision rule: If core, bias toward build (with targeted partner support). If enabling, buy and configure.

2) Urgency and time-to-value

What is the real cost of waiting - revenue, share, cost structure, customer trust? Can you afford 12–18 months to ship and learn?

Decision rule: Need results in less than 6 months → buy. You can invest 12–18 months → consider building.

3) Current technical capabilities

Do you currently have production-grade ML talent and data engineers? Is your data clean, tagged, and accessible through governed APIs? Do you have evals, monitoring, and incident playbooks defined?

Decision rule: Missing **two or more** of the above → **buy**. Strong foundation → **consider build**.

4) Budget reality

What can you fund over three years, including maintenance, governance, and iteration? Market evidence suggests that deployments of six figures or more are common; however, DIY typically carries higher variance and a longer payback period.

Decision rule: Constrained or uncertain budget → buy. Flexible multi-year funding → consider building.

5) Long-term strategic vision

Is building internal AI capability a multi-year priority? Will you reuse the platform across multiple systems? Are you willing to learn through controlled failure?

Decision rule: One-off initiative → **buy**. Journey to an AI Center of Excellence → **build (phased)**.

A Practical Build vs. Buy Decision Matrix

Scenario	Build Score	Buy Score	Recommendation
AI is core + strong internal capability + flexible timeline	HIGH	LOW	Build (with professional consultation)
AI enables core functions + limited capability + <6 months urgency	LOW	HIGH	Buy
AI differentiator + some capability + moderate urgency	MEDIUM	MEDIUM	Hybrid: buy & customize
Utility function + no capability + tight budget	LOW	HIGH	Buy
Strategic investment + building capability + long timeline	HIGH	MEDIUM	Phased: buy then build

Red flags for DIY

Proceed with extreme caution if:

- you have zero in-house AI/ML expertise;
- your data governance is weak;
- your timeline is less than 6 months;
- your budget is volatile;
- executive sponsorship is tentative.

What to ask Professional Partners

To evaluate a professional implementation partner, you need to confirm that they can deliver production-ready solutions in your environment on time, within scope, and hand over operations to your team. Ask each partner the same questions and request proof:

Experience & expertise: How many agentic deployments to production? In our industry? What is your production success rate and your average time to value? How do you handle data quality gaps?

Methodology: Show your implementation playbook - requirements, governance checkpoints, evaluation harness, and knowledge transfer. How do you manage scope changes and run post-deployment optimization?

Cost & timeline: What are typical ranges for projects like ours? What's included vs. not? Fixed-price or value-based options?

Team: Who is on our squad, how senior are they, and how much of **our** team's time is required?

Answers here are more predictive of success than any slide on "AI vision."

The Hybrid Path Forward

Hybrid is the practical default for most companies. You buy a stable platform and core components. You bring in a professional partner to ship the first production system. You grow a small internal team while the system goes live. The aim is speed now and control later.

Why Most Organizations Choose Hybrid

The MIT reporting is clear: programs that purchase core tools and partner for implementation materially outperform internal green-field builds in terms of success rate and speed to measurable impact. Taking the hybrid approach is not some compromise or fence-sitting. In most cases, the appropriate strategy is to buy the proven substrate and then build your differentiators on top.

A Phased Capability Build

- **Phase 1 — Partner-led (Months 1–6):** Ship the first production system with a professional partner. Make value proof the goal, not model cleverness. Establish governance, logging, and an evaluation loop (see Chapter 9).
- **Phase 2 — Collaborative (Months 7–12):** Co-develop the second wave. Your team assumes more ownership. Start your internal Center of Excellence and codify playbooks.
- **Phase 3 — Internal-led (Month 13+):** Your team leads net-new builds; partners supply specialist help, benchmarking, and architectural reviews. Your differentiators live here.

What to Build Internally

Invest in AI literacy across roles. Hire for keystone skills (ML engineers, data engineers, evaluation/QA for AI, prompt/retrieval specialists). Partner for cutting-edge domains (safety, compliance, emerging frameworks). Write and maintain internal playbooks because your process knowledge will become compounding IP over time.

Making your decision

A 10-point self-assessment

Use the checklist that follows as a quick gate review with your CFO and head of engineering. Answer each line Yes or No. Then apply the rules of thumb below. The goal is clarity you can act on today.

How to use the checklist (rules of thumb):

- **If any of the first three are No** (objectives, capability, and data quality; 3-year TCO), **pause the build**. Choose **buy** or **hybrid** for now.
- **If you have around 4–6 Yeses** and you need results inside six months, then **Buy**.
- **If you have around 6–8 Yeses** and AI is **not** your core differentiator, **Buy with customization** or go **Hybrid**.

- **If you have around 8–10 Yeses** and AI is core to your edge, **plan a Build**, ideally with targeted partner support.

Now work through the 10 points below:

- Objectives are clear and quantified
- Technical capability and data quality are honestly assessed
- 3-year TCO is modeled for both paths
- Time-to-value needs are explicit
- AI's role in competitive advantage is agreed
- Budget and risk tolerance are aligned
- Candidate partners are evaluated
- Executive sponsorship is secured
- Success metrics and ROI method are defined
- Governance (safety/compliance/observability) is in scope from day one

Recommended Build, Buy, or Hybrid Development Path by Organization Type

Organization Type	Recommended Path	Rationale
Startups & SMBs	Buy	You need speed, not a research lab. Focus scarce resources on product and customers. Add hybrid later after repeatable value.
Mid-market	Buy with customization or Hybrid	Some engineering strength but limited specialized AI depth. Optimize for time-to-value while building internal capability alongside partners.
Enterprises	Hybrid or Selective Build	Mix portfolio: buy for utility and integration-heavy workflows; build only truly differentiating capabilities. Many start with partners to accelerate first wins and de-risk governance.

Your next steps

If you're choosing to buy/partner:

1. Document requirements and outcome metrics in business terms. Specify use case, users, data sources, systems to integrate, constraints (security, privacy, compliance), and success metrics.

2. Shortlist 3–5 partners with live customer deployments.
3. Request proposals with scope, timeline, price, and an AI governance plan.
4. Check references of current and former clients. Confirm the time to first value, scope, timeline, integrations, security, and support. Ask if they would rehire.
5. Run a 4–6 week pilot with a clear success bar and exit criteria (Chapter 12).
6. Include knowledge transfer and internal capability ramp-up in the Statement of Work (SOW).

If you're choosing to build:

1. Run a readiness check on the team, data, access, and integrations, and record any gaps with the owners and corresponding dates.
2. Draft an 18–24 month hiring and training plan anchored to the roadmap.
3. Fund data plumbing and governance first.
4. Stand up evaluation and monitoring early.
5. Ship the smallest viable production-ready AI version of your application (not a demo) and instrument it.
6. Commission architecture reviews from external experts at key project milestones: before the pilot, before production, and before scale.
7. Expect and plan for timeline slips and budget variances; manage scope effectively.

If you're choosing hybrid:

1. Buy proven components and safety/observability layers.
2. Build your differentiators.
3. Select a partner for the first wave to compress time-to-value.
4. Run a structured knowledge-transfer plan.
5. Hire and train for sustainability.
6. Transition ownership over 12–18 months.

Conclusion: The decision that shapes your AI future

The weight of current evidence suggests that most internal-only AI applications' building approaches stall not because people aren't smart, but because AI systems are socio-technical and the integration/governance burden is heavy. The build vs. buy call should follow a plain rule: buy the proven base and partner to ship now; build in-house later only where it strengthens your moat.

Executives who win combine pragmatism and ambition. They buy a proven base platform to get working systems into production quickly. They partner so their team learns and adopts the workflows and controls to run the system in production. And they build only where they can defend a moat with proprietary data, process, or brand. Done this way, the hybrid path becomes your on-ramp to a genuine AI capability. Your board will back it, your teams can operate it, and your customers will notice the change.

Choose whether you build, buy, or adopt a hybrid approach to AI with your eyes wide open. Programs that use partners reach production faster and more often. Internal-only efforts often stall or get cut. In AI, success follows the teams that execute, measure, and learn, not the teams that romanticize a build for AI's sake.

References:

- The Root Causes of Failure for Artificial Intelligence Projects and How They Can Succeed: Avoiding the Anti-Patterns of AI | RAND
- AI project failure rates are on the rise: report | CIO Dive
- Gartner Predicts 30% of Generative AI Projects Will Be Abandoned After Proof of Concept By End of 2025
- MIT report: 95% of generative AI pilots at companies are failing | Fortune
- Superagency in the workplace: Empowering people to unlock AI's full potential
- The Root Causes of Failure for Artificial Intelligence Projects and How They Can Succeed: Avoiding the Anti-Patterns of AI
- Widening talent gap threatens executives' AI ambitions – Bain & Company
- AI skills gap widens. | Randstad
- Skills-based hiring is driving salary premiums in the AI sector as employers face talent shortage, Oxford study finds
- AI Skills Gap | IBM
- Build vs Buy AI: Which Choice Saves You Money in 2025?
- Enterprise AI Services: Build vs. Buy Framework | HP® Tech Takes
- AI Implementation Roadmap: 6-Phase Guide for 2025

CHAPTER 12

Your First 4-Week Pilot Program

Few AI pilots deliver all their intended business results. This is an uncomfortable truth of the IT industry. In 2025, MIT researchers reported that about 95% of generative AI pilots fail to deliver meaningful business results. The reasons are almost always the same: program goals are too vague, success metrics are undefined, the outcome is not aligned with the function or business strategy, the AI technology built is a fragile prototype not yet production-ready, or there is no plan for what comes after the pilot phase.

The good news is that the inverse is also true. The pilots who succeed follow a disciplined approach. They tie a narrow AI use case to measurable outcomes, build on top of production-grade foundations, and insist that third-party teams transfer operating knowledge to an internal team that will own the AI system in the future. This helps to ensure the pilot phase builds enduring internal capability, avoiding a never-ending black-box dependency on external partners for technical support.

This chapter highlights how to get definitive evidence of a pilot's viability in just one month, while laying the tram tracks for future AI programs to scale on top.

What this chapter does: it shows how to generate decision-grade evidence in four weeks and lays the track for scale. Chapter 11 helped you choose whether to build, buy, or take a hybrid path. This chapter sets the operating cadence for that choice. If you decide to partner or buy an agentic platform, you will need to understand where external partners can add speed, what your internal team must own, and how to measure everyone's progress each and every week.

Similarly, if you choose to build your own team to support your agent, this chapter provides you with a management tool to mitigate the risks associated with that choice. This chapter will quickly tell you if you have the right team, the right plan, and a realistic chance of success.

Why Pilots Fail and the Blueprint for Success

Most AI pilots stall for three reasons: the absence of a clear problem statement, no agreed success KPIs or measurements, or a lack of suitable production-optimized infrastructure.

Of course, there are organizational factors such as a lack of management buy-in, talent gaps, or unrealistic budgets and expectations, which can undermine the success of your pilot. These topics are discussed in detail in Chapter 11. For the purposes of this chapter, we assume that once you commence a pilot, the organizational prerequisites are in place and the primary obstacles that remain are technical and structural.

You cannot manage what you don't measure, and you can't scale code that was never designed to run in production. The fixes are straightforward:

- Treat a pilot as a 4-week production-ready version of your agentic AI system, not a disposable lab demo.
- Define 3–5 business KPIs on Day 1. Each KPI should have a baseline, a target, and a measurement method. Instrument the pilot so that the dashboard updates daily. Organizations that revise their KPI systems with AI are three times more likely to report greater financial benefits than those that do not.
- Define a ruthless, minimalist scope. The goal of an AI pilot program is not to build an entire production-ready AI system; it's to answer a single, critical business question. For example, if your goal is to prove the agent can reduce response times, integrate *only* with the email and ticketing systems. Defer every other "nice-to-have" feature, such as a knowledge base integration or a fancy UI, until after the pilot has proven its core value.
- Involve line leadership paired with executive sponsorship. Top-down AI initiatives might struggle to gain traction if management is not sufficiently involved. McKinsey finds that 68% of managers have recommended a gen-AI tool to solve a team problem in the last month, and 86% of those recommendations worked. This is a powerful "bottom-up" energy. Give these managers a formal role in an AI pilot program and harness their momentum to drive the AI program forward within the organization.

  Conversely, bottom-up initiatives won't stick without top-down air cover. Name an executive sponsor to secure the budget, clear blockers, and set decision rights. A dual partnership involving business line champions, along with executive backing, drives adoption within the organization.
- If you partner with an AI specialist organization to co-build your agentic pilot, insist on knowledge transfer from day one. External expertise can accelerate an AI build process, but your team must be able to operate the system after Week 4. Make it a contractual requirement for a partner's experts to train your team *during* a pilot. There shouldn't only be a small 30-page document handed over in Week 4. Your engineers ought to be doing daily code pairing sessions with the external partner's engineers, participating in code reviews, and getting hands-on experience with the architecture from day one.

A final note on partnerships: recent BCG research finds that organizations that combine internal teams with external vendors report higher program satisfaction, clearer ROI tracking, and greater cost savings. Additionally, a diverse partner ecosystem accelerates GenAI performance by allowing you to focus on innovation, rather than reinvention. Avoid rebuilding foundational components under deadline pressure; use mature tools and patterns that already work. You are not handing your future to a vendor. You are utilizing outside experts to expedite shipping while your team learns the operating patterns for integration, governance, and safety.

The 4 Week Structure at a Glance

Week 1: Discovery, design, and alignment. Align stakeholders on a single use case, a crisp business outcome statement, and a measurement plan. Draft the "thin slice" architecture: a small, end-to-end version of the system that shows how the parts connect and work together. Then line up the data sources for that first version so the team can begin building with real input. You should end Week 1 with a signed one-page scope and a KPI dashboard mock-up.

Week 2: Core development with production foundations. Build the smallest set of capabilities in your AI pilot that can move the KPI needle. The ship works in increments every few days. Instrument for monitoring from the start. Pair your partner's engineers with your own to begin skills transfer.

Week 3: Integration, testing, and optimization. Wire the agent to the one or two systems it needs to interact with. Run structured user testing with a small group. Remove the rough edges that block adoption. Measure cost, quality, and latency with the same rigor you apply to conventional software.

Week 4: Deployment, measurement, and the scale decision. Roll out to a controlled user population. Watch the dashboards daily. Capture evidence against the success bar and make a Go / Conditional Go / No-Go call. If you have reached project Go status, leave Week 4 with a 60–90 day scale plan and named owners against actions.

Week 1: Discovery, design, and alignment

Week 1 should prevent the three most common failure modes: unclear scope, mismatched expectations, and unmeasured value. You are not selecting a grand challenge. You are choosing a sharp problem with accessible data, a visible business owner, and a clear way to measure improvement in thirty days. Think one team, one workflow, one or two systems, and a short list of metrics.

Start with interviews and a short workshop that includes the people who feel the problem in their day-to-day work, the manager who owns the process, the technical lead who owns the relevant systems, and the partner's lead architect, if they are using one. Map the current flow and identify the time sinks, error traps, and hand-offs. Pick a single bottleneck that is both painful and measurable.

Lock the outcomes before the architecture. Write a one-paragraph value hypothesis, such as:

"Within four weeks, the agent should reduce average response time to inbound Tier-1 support tickets from 24 hours to 4 hours for the pilot group, handle at least 40% of Tier-1 tickets end-to-end, and sustain an 80% user satisfaction score."

Then convert that paragraph into a small set of KPI definitions with baselines, targets, and collection methods. For many organizations, Google Cloud's guide to gen-AI KPIs serves as a useful scaffold that distinguishes technical metrics (latency, accuracy), operational metrics (cycle time, rework), and business metrics (cost per case, retention) and shows how to instrument them.

Design the minimal end-to-end version. Please keep it simple and stable. Confirm data sources, integration points, and identity requirements. Decide upfront how you will log prompts, responses, and errors, as well as how you will track costs. Sketch guardrails for content safety and escalation. You are designing the first version of a system that can run next month, not the system that will serve your full enterprise next year.

End Week 1 with four concrete artifacts:

1. **One-page scope** that names the use case, the in-scope user stories, and the out-of-scope requests you will defer.
2. **KPI sheet** with baselines, targets, and methods of measurement.
3. **An architecture sketch** that shows data sources, integrations, security boundaries, and monitoring hooks.
4. **The working plan for Week 2 and Week 3** with owners and calendar holds for daily standups and end-of-week reviews.

Week-1 checklist

- Objectives and success criteria are written in business language and agreed upon.
- Stakeholders and decision rights are explicit.
- Data availability and access are confirmed.
- Risks and assumptions are documented.
- The team knows what "done" would look like on Day 28.

Pilots that start with locked KPIs and a simple measurement plan avoid the false choice between "fast" and "rigorous." As MIT Sloan/BCG shows, organizations that upgrade KPI practices report far better financial outcomes, because they steer with evidence rather than opinion.

Week 2: Core development with production foundations

Week 2 focuses on building a narrow capability that works effectively while laying the robust foundations needed for production. Think in short, inspectable increments. Many teams utilize one-week sprints, with daily 15-minute stand-ups and end-of-week reviews. If you work with a professional partner, seat your developers next to theirs and pair on real tickets. You want the flow of knowledge as much as the flow of code.

Start by standing up the data path. Ingest the minimal data required for the thin slice, adhering to hygiene rules and ensuring observability. Next, implement the agent's core flow for the primary user story. Keep tool integrations to the essentials. For example, a customer support agent might integrate only with the ticketing system this week and defer knowledge base search until Week 3 if you can still test the value hypothesis without it.

From the first commit, treat instrumentation and reliability as first-class work: log prompts and responses, capture errors with stack traces, and tag interactions to the pilot to separate pilot metrics from the rest of the business. Add safety guardrails appropriate to the use case. Document as you go. These disciplines prevent the "we'll productionize it later" trap that kills many pilots.

Two additional Week-2 practices pay dividends:

- **Frequent demos.** Show rough edges to business users two or three times this week. You are tuning for usefulness, not for a perfect UX.
- **Pairing for transfer.** Ask your partner to schedule daily pairing blocks and an end-of-week architecture walkthrough. Your engineers should be able to explain how the agent works and where to look when something breaks.

Week-2 deliverables

- A working demo for the core use case, instrumented and observable.
- Minimal integrations to exercise the value hypothesis.
- Logging, monitoring, and a basic safety layer are in place.
- Draft runbook and dependency list.

The success rate for AI initiatives rises when teams reuse hard-won patterns around integration, safety, and measurement rather than inventing them. External partners introduce these patterns; your team must now absorb them so that Week 4 does not end with a black-box system.

Week 3: Integration, testing, and optimization

With the core path live, Week 3 moves from demo use to production use. Connect the agent to a minimal live system with one or two core components that make the pilot real. Keep a tight list: authentication and access, the workflow system you decided on in Week 1, and any read-only knowledge sources you must query.

Then shift into structured user testing. Recruit a small pilot group and script realistic scenarios that include happy paths and messy edge cases. Measure the same KPIs you set in Week 1, and add usability notes: where people hesitate, where they try to click the wrong thing, where the agent is confident but wrong. Track cost, latency, and error rates day by day. Optimize the obvious bottlenecks. For many pilots, small prompt refinements, clearer escalation rules, and lightweight caching reduce costs and improve user trust.

Maintain the operating tempo:

- Daily standups against a short wall of defects and improvements.
- End-of-week review with the business owner to confirm progress against the success bar.
- Documentation updates and short enablement sessions for the support team.

By the end of Week 3, the pilot should be fully integrated, safe to expose to a limited user, and 0% of target KPIs, population, and instrumented to show whether it is hitting the mark.

Week-3 checklist

- Integration points tested end-to-end with error handling.
- User acceptance testing completed with structured feedback.
- Performance and cost benchmarks captured.
- Training materials drafted for pilot users.
- Rollout gates and rollback plan drafted for Week 4.

Week 4: Deployment, measurement, and the scale decision

Week 4 is where the pilot earns its keep. Roll out to a controlled user group. Keep the group small enough to watch closely and large enough to generate a signal. Activate the implementation and KPI dashboards (*outlined in Chapter 10*) and monitor them daily, focusing on technical metrics (uptime, latency), operational metrics (cycle time, rework), and the business outcome that matters most to you.

Communicate with stakeholders every morning via a brief note: what happened yesterday, what we learned, and what we will change today.

Run a tight issue-triage ritual: one owner for user feedback, one for incidents, one for metrics. Publish fixes quickly. Because you instrumented the system from Day 1, you can separate anecdotes from evidence.

By day 26 or 27, shift to decision framing. Summarize the evidence against your Week-1 targets and prepare a simple Go / Conditional Go / No-Go recommendation:

- **Go** — You achieved most targets, users are positive, the system is stable, risks are understood, and there is a clear path to ROI.
- **Conditional Go** — Mixed results; you need 2–4 weeks of iteration to clear specific issues, or you will scale to a second cohort while you complete hardening work.
- **No-Go** — You learned something valuable, but the current approach does not justify expansion. Capture lessons and propose a pivot or shutdown.

Close Week 4 with two artifacts:

1. **A pilot results brief** that shows KPI achievement, adoption, technical posture, risks, and lessons learned.
2. **60–90 day scale plan** with named owners. The plan should state the next target population, incremental integrations, resilience work, and the governance model for changes.

Pilots that go quiet at the finish line die in committee. Pilots that arrive with daily evidence, crisp trade-offs, and a scale plan get funded.

The Go / Conditional Go / No-Go decision, defined

Keep the decision rules visible from Day 1. The following thresholds are practical and defensible:

- **Go** when you meet at least 70% of target KPIs, achieve 80%+ satisfaction among pilot users, demonstrate stability under expected load, and show a clear path to unit economics that beats today's process.
- **Conditional Go** when results are mixed but tractable: for example, latency is within target, but accuracy requires another sprint, or adoption is strong, but one integration needs to be hardened.

- **No-Go** when the KPI story does not hold, a critical risk remains unresolved, or the value hypothesis proves wrong. Stopping is considered a success if it saves you from a costly scale-out.

Week-4 decision pack checklist

- KPI dashboard with actual vs. target and commentary. One page that displays each metric you set in Week 1, including the baseline, target, and actual results. Add a short note on why a metric is above or below target and what you will change next.
- User adoption and satisfaction summary with quotes and examples. A simple view of who used it, how often, and what they thought. Include a short survey score, usage counts by day, and two or three verbatim quotes that capture the experience.
- Technical posture: stability, safety, cost per transaction, and known risks.
- Scale plan: next population, added integrations, resilience and governance work, budget envelope, and owners.

Investment and the resource ask

Executives expect a budget frame. Use conservative ranges and keep the split transparent. Vendor estimates commonly place small-business pilots in the \$50,000–\$150,000 range, with large enterprise programs rising into the millions as scope expands. Four-week pilots on a single workflow typically land near the lower end of that spectrum when you use mature platforms and a focused partner.

Internal time asks for a credible 4-week run:

- Executive sponsor: 5–10 hours per week for decisions and unblockers.
- Product owner or line manager: ~50% to drive priorities and adoption.
- Two to four engineers (partnered with external specialists if applicable): 50–100% for build, test, and ops.
- SMEs from the business: 10–20 hours over the month for interviews, testing, and training.

This is the smallest unit that can do meaningful work fast without burning out the same two people who already keep the lights on.

Risk controls and common traps

Scope creep is the fastest way to hit Week 4 with nothing to show. Keep a living out-of-scope list and enforce it. Data surprises can scupper pilots when teams discover governance policies late; ensure data access requests are completed in Week 1. Prototype-only code creates a rebuild tax; avoid it by wiring logging, monitoring, and safety on Day 1. Stakeholder drift is often a problem, so maintain weekly reviews tied to the KPI sheet to ensure alignment.

Week-by-week guidance summarized

By the end of Week 1, you have a one-page scope, a signed KPI sheet, data access, and a thin-slice architecture. You know exactly what you are testing and how you will measure it. You have daily and weekly cadences booked.

During Week 2, you move from paper to working software. Ship the happy path, start observing real signals, and capture early user feedback. The system is instrumented, not a black box.

As Week 3 begins, you integrate with the minimum set of live systems, run user acceptance testing with a small pilot group, and optimize the areas where the metrics indicate friction or underperformance. You also finalize training guides and support runbooks.

In Week 4, you run a controlled rollout, measure your progress against the targets, and make the scaling decision. If it is **Go**, conclude the pilot with a 60–90 day scaling plan, clear next steps, and designated owners for each workstream. If it is a Conditional Go, you schedule the follow-up work and align with leadership in a quick follow-up meeting to validate progress before scaling. If it is No-Go, you close with a tight lesson-learned brief and redeploy resources.

Conclusion: What success looks like

A good pilot is not a demo. It is a verified change in a business metric for a named cohort of users; along with the bare bones of a system you can scale. Typical outcomes in four weeks include measurable improvements in cycle time or first-contact resolution, a credible cost-per-transaction, and evidence that users prefer the new path once rough edges are removed. Adoption matters. Managers are already recommending tools and seeing them work. Use that energy. Do not try to convince skeptics with slogans; convince them with results that are instrumented.

A four-week pilot is not about proving that AI is exciting. It is about proving, or disproving, a specific business result quickly and cleanly, then using that evidence to decide what comes next. Run your AI pilot with clear metrics, production discipline, and daily communication. Do that, and you give your organization something rare in AI: a short, certain step toward outcomes that last.

References:

- Why 95% of AI Pilots Fail, And What Business Leaders Should Do Instead
- The Future of Strategic Measurement: Enhancing KPIs With AI
- KPIs for gen AI: Measuring your AI success | Google Cloud Blog
- Superagency in the workplace: Empowering people to unlock AI's full potential
- How to Collaborate with Vendors to Maximize GenAI Impact | BCG
- AI Implementation Roadmap: 6-Phase Guide for 2025

CHAPTER 13

Your Personalized AI Implementation Roadmap

Why you need a personalized AI roadmap

AI only compounds impact when it is steered like a system or program, not sprinkled like glitter. AI adoption in businesses globally is growing, yet consistent value still clusters among a small group of high-performing companies that run multiple scaled AI use cases, invest with intent, and treat risk management as a product requirement.

At this point, the decision between building, buying, or using a hybrid choice, as outlined in Chapter 11, has already been made. You've shipped a pilot and are capturing baseline KPIs. The next step is not to add more system features but to scale AI outcomes with discipline.

Industry data shows movement without scale is a common business problem. AI has been widely adopted (approximately 72% of businesses have adopted some form of AI). Still, only a relatively small number of companies (approximately 46 out of 876 respondents) reported they saw a substantial impact on EBIT from their AI investments.

McKinsey's 2024 research found that while organizations are embracing AI more broadly, value is increasingly concentrated on operating models and governance as AI technology advances.

A comparative analysis has shown that significant business results can be achieved when companies redesign their work processes by utilizing AI to transform business workflows. Less successful companies tend not to attempt to scale AI. Instead, they adopt AI in isolated business units or automate small business tasks.

Overall, AI service-operations studies reveal a significant execution gap between successful and less successful adopters of AI. The harsh fact business leaders face today is that there are relatively few firms running multiple scaled use cases across their core business operations.

The message from all these industry reports is that scale AI requires an operating model; merely having a stack of polished tech tools will not suffice. This chapter outlines the operating model. We will demonstrate how to run the program in three parts: early-phase setup, a few continuously executing core feedback and delivery loops, and domain-level decision gates.

Phase 1: Readiness and Operating Model

Run the Agentic Readiness Assessment (ARA)

The purpose of a readiness assessment is to establish a baseline, so the AI plan aligns with your current reality. The ARA supplements the pilot scorecard, previously outlined in Chapter 12, and serves as the executive dashboard for the next 6 to 18 months.

How to score: rate each dimension on a 0–5 scale with evidence, not opinion.

1. **Business clarity:** Are AI program outcomes tied to P&L or mission, and is there a single accountable executive for each use case?
2. **Data readiness:** Do teams have policy-compliant access to the right data with acceptable quality and latency?
3. **Architecture and platform:** Do you have secure runtime, observability, model access, and reliable application or system integrations that meet required service levels?
4. **People and skills:** Do product owners, subject-matter experts, agent engineers, and integration engineers have time to work on the program, and are their roles clearly defined?
5. **Governance and risk:** Are policies and controls in place for model inventory, data lineage, bias testing, monitoring, and incident response? Use the AI TRiSM (*Trust, Risk & Security Management*) lens as a checklist (IBM Think: What is AI TRiSM).
6. **Change and adoption.** Are line managers engaged, training plans in place, and champions identified? Can telemetry be set up to track adoption and usage (active users, task success, satisfaction, unit cost)?
7. **Economics.** Are the KPI baselines and unit costs known, along with the budget envelope and target return on investment?

Process: Typically, two to three weeks of interviews and artifact review are sufficient. Produce a heat map, list fast fixes versus structural gaps, and link each gap to a remediation track. Treat the ARA like a health check that you will repeat at each major gate.

Output: A one-page readiness profile with three elements: a color-coded score by dimension, a written summary of the top three bottlenecks, and a remediation plan with owners and dates. Keep it visible in every executive review.

Build the operating model that sustains scale

Technology is necessary but not sufficient. Leaders who scale AI treat AI like a managed product portfolio, not a series of small experiments. Two patterns dominate here. You can blend them, but pick one as primary:

1. **Hub-and-Spoke.** A central platform and governance team owns reusable components, risk controls, and standards. Business spokes own demand, outcomes, and adoption.
2. **Product-line Pods.** Cross-functional squads own a domain end-to-end. The platform team functions as a product and serves pods with secure, reliable shared services.

Whatever you choose, name decision rights. Each domain should have an AI Product Owner, a Data Owner, and a Risk Signatory. Give them time to work on the program and authority to make decisions.

Below are the decision rights that matter:

- Who approves the use case intake?
- Who sets and evolves standards for prompts, evals, and safety?
- Who can gate a release on reliability or risk findings?
- Who owns the resourcing and budget by quarter?

Performance improves when accountability is situated close to the work, and leaders review progress at a predictable cadence.

Codify the playbook. Version prompts and agents. Insist on an evaluation suite and a rollback plan for every release. Log every code change, including a clear reason and the owner's name. Treat runbooks and test harnesses as living documents.

Phase 2: Portfolio and Anchor Plan

Rank your opportunities by impact and complexity

You need a portfolio view, not a list of favorites. Use a simple Impact × Complexity matrix and score 1-5 on each axis.

- **Impact** considers revenue lift, cost reduction, risk reduction, and customer experience. Pick one primary value driver per use case to prevent muddled goals.

- **Complexity** is considered in terms of data availability, the number of systems to integrate, workflow changes, and compliance risk. Add a "policy sensitivity" note for any use case that touches regulated content.

The impact-complexity matrix should be tempered with reality checks:

- Define impact as a measurable improvement tied to a KPI and define complexity as a blend of delivery cost and risk.
- Add a confidence column to your backlog. If you're unsure about an estimate, treat it as a lower priority until the evidence improves.
- Annotate hard dependencies so that your quick win is not blocked by a long-forgotten platform code change.
- Keep the impact-complexity prioritization grid lightweight. Use it to make the first ten calls, not to create false precision.

Choose an Anchor Domain to Harvest Reusability

Select a business area where several related use cases can share data, tools, and teams. Focusing on this one anchor allows you to reuse platforms, governance, and change management, making each subsequent use case faster and more cost-effective.

Examples:

- **Customer support as the anchor:**

  Wave 1: agent assist summarization → Wave 2: knowledge search → Wave 3: auto-classification.

  Reused assets: include the customer data connector, RAG index, policy guardrails, and QA workflow.

- **Accounts payable as the anchor:**

  Wave 1: invoice extraction → Wave 2: 3-way match assistance → Wave 3: vendor inquiry bot.

  Reused assets: include the document pipeline, validation rules, and approval controls.

Phase 3: Pathway and quarter roadmap

Choose your implementation pathway

Your ARA score and pilot results guide the path ahead. Each path assumes that you carry forward the production bones from Chapter 12, rather than discarding them.

Path A: High-Readiness (12 weeks after the pilot)

Best suited for: organizations scoring four or higher in data, platform, governance, and adoption.

Objective: scale the pilot domain and stand up a second domain by week twelve.

Timeline and milestones

- **Weeks 1–2.** Finalize the scale plan for the pilot domain. Expand integrations and operational volume (more users, cases, and data throughput) to test scale under real load. Confirm governance and sign owners in risk and privacy. Staff cross-functional pods with a product owner, SME, agent engineer, integration engineer, QA, designer, and a risk liaison. Reconfirm KPI targets and unit economics assumptions.
- **Weeks 3–6.** Harden production. Migrate early users, expand to the full department, and hold weekly operational reviews. Watch three dials: success rate by task, mean time to completion, and cost per transaction. Treat them as your control panel for making go/hold/rollback decisions each week and for determining the next set of fixes.
- **Weeks 7–12.** Launch a second domain. Reuse components like prompt templates, data connections, guardrails/policies, test checks, and the deploy/monitor setup, etc., from the first weeks. Publish a versioned, access-controlled shared AI library (v1.0) with named owners and a simple change process**,** so that teams can adopt it without re-approval. Release a short "How we build agents here" playbook that spells out steps, roles, gates, and what "done" means.

Checkpoints

- **Gate 1.** Governance controls pass. KPI baselines and targets are signed.
- **Gate 2.** Service levels are maintained in production, and the cost-per-transaction trend is in the right direction.
- **Gate 3.** The second domain pilot has met the exit criteria and is approved for rollout.

Path B: Medium-Readiness (8 weeks of prep, then 16 weeks of scale)

Best suited for: organizations with mixed scores (two to three) on data plumbing, governance, or adoption.

Objective: shore up the long poles and then scale the pilot domain.

Prep phase: eight weeks

- Fix data access and quality bottlenecks in the data path.
- Stand up model inventory, data lineage, and monitoring.
- Convert your KPI hypotheses into a living dashboard that reports both the baseline (e.g., current success rate, time to completion, cost per transaction) for each KPI and the target, not just snapshots. The Google KPI tree reference helps teams produce clean, comparable views (Gen-AI KPIs).
- Develop a user adoption plan that enables managers and champions to effectively guide their teams in utilizing the new AI tools. Commit to weekly usage reviews to review participation data (e.g., number of active users, task success rates, and user feedback) and identify where extra support or adjustments are needed.

Scale phase: sixteen weeks

- Expand the pilot domain with a small, dedicated team responsible for scaling and operating the AI use case, while the platform team reinforces shared data, governance, and infrastructure services.
- Add a second pod at mid-point if service levels and governance controls are stable.
- Publish a short release policy for prompts and agents. Treat them like software: keep versions, test each release, and monitor quality and unit cost. If a new version lowers quality or pushes cost over the limit, roll back to the previous version.

Checkpoints

- **Prep gate.** Governance and data controls are ready. Adoption plans are approved.
- **Midpoint gate.** Progress is at least 70% toward the pilot's stated KPI goals. The unit cost of the service in this domain (e.g., per resolved case, per generated document, or per query) exhibits a clear downward trend and remains within the planned budget.
- **Exit gate.** Expand to a second domain with shared components and runbooks.

Path C: Early-Stage (six months of foundation, then pilot and scale)

Who it fits: organizations scoring two or below in multiple dimensions. Data is fragmented, governance is light, and staffing is thin. No dedicated product owner; limited data and platform engineering; small QA and operations capacity; and no named risk/privacy or change-management partner, often part-time.

Objective: Set up the core platform, data access, security/privacy controls, testing, monitoring, and deployment. Prove it with a focused pilot, then scale it up.

Foundation: six months

- Establish governance controls across the pilot lifecycle. Create an inventory of every model and use case, listing the owner, purpose, data sources, where it runs, approvals, last review date, and maintain a change log. Introduce bias testing and red-team exercises. Align incident response with company security and privacy standards.
- Stand up platform basics: retrieval, policy guardrails, monitoring, and cost telemetry.
- Create a small agent toolkit with evaluation harnesses and human-in-the-loop controls.
- Train champions and publish KPI templates.

Pilot: four weeks

- Re-run the Chapter 12 pilot method on a narrow use case. Treat it as a prove-the-rails engagement. The deliverable is not only a working agent, but also a comprehensive solution. It is proof that policy, monitoring, security, and rollback work at production speed.

Scale: twelve to sixteen weeks

- Roll out to the department with one pod. Add a second only after stability has been maintained for 30 days.

Checkpoints

- **Foundation gate:** Policy and platform controls verified.
- **Pilot gate:** KPI targets met and incident drills complete.
- **Scale gate:** Service levels and cost stability have been consistently demonstrated over a thirty-day period.

Putting it together: one-page roadmaps executives can approve

Each domain should carry a single page that captures scope, timeline, budget envelope, KPIs, risks, and named owners. It should be designed to fit on a page without requiring layout tweaks or font resizing. Use this one-page roadmap to frame every decision gate. Update it monthly. Retire the one-page roadmap when the domain is in a steady state (day-to-day operation).

Loops – Continuous Activities

Loops here mean the work you run on a rhythm. Loops do not finish; they repeat weekly and monthly to keep the program healthy between big decision points. Loops run in parallel across domains and feed the gates (decision checkpoints) with fresh data.

Governance six-check verification

Trust and risk are not side projects. They are table stakes for scaling AI. Make governance, safety, and compliance part of how you build, not an afterthought. Move the controls into automated pipelines and dashboards so they run by default.

Track whether the following controls are in place (For more details on how to build and run the guardrails, incidents, audits, etc., see Chapter 9):

1. **Model inventory and lineage:** Know what is in production, why it was changed, and who approved it.
2. **Data controls:** Ensure permissions, retention, and redaction are enforced through code and policy.
3. **Bias and misuse testing:** Have a small team try to “break” the system with risky or unfair prompts.
4. **Track a simple scoreboard:** tests run, tests failed, what failed (bias, privacy, unsafe advice), and severity. Fix the issues and retest as with any other quality defect.
5. **Runtime monitoring:** Track code quality, drift, error classes, and safety incidents.
6. **Incident response:** Define a pathway from a user report to a mitigation strategy and a release process.
7. **Audit trails:** Log decision making. Keep evidence for compliance reviews.

Portfolio KPIs and Economics on one page per domain

Leaders need a one-page management summary for each business domain that summarizes three key elements: outcomes, unit economics, and reliability.

1. **Outcomes:** The two or three KPIs that matter, tied to P&L or mission. Show baseline, current, and delta. If the KPI is too slow, include a predictive leading indicator.
2. **Unit economics:** Show the cost per completed AI-assisted task or customer interaction (for example, cost per resolved support case, per qualified lead, or per generated document), or whatever cost metric best fits the business domain. Include a simple trend line so leaders can see whether costs are improving over time.
3. **Reliability:** Borrow the SRE playbook. Define service level indicators (SLIs) and service level objectives (SLOs) that matter to users, plus an error budget that determines release velocity. This removes business politics from the question of "is it reliable enough to expand?" See Google SRE's free, canonical guidance on SLOs and error budgets.

   SLIs = the measurements you track;

   SLOs = the targets for those measurements;

   Error budget = the allowed misses before you slow releases.

Deliverable: A laminated single-pager per domain with three boxes: results, economics, and reliability. Leaders should be able to review ten of these in fifteen minutes.

Resourcing and Cadence

Put people where the work is stuck, not where the org chart says they should be. For every two pods delivering in your anchor domain (i.e., the first business area chosen to prove value and build reusable components), plan roughly a half-pod for platform work, and add a named risk partner who understands the controls you use. Keep the rhythm simple and steady: hold weekly outcome reviews in each pod; every two weeks, run a reuse review across teams to determine which prompts, tools, data connectors, and tests should be included in the shared kit; and conduct a monthly portfolio review with the executive sponsor.

When in doubt, narrow the scope and ship smaller updates more often. Value grows when AI is integrated into more functions, and the team adheres to a dependable weekly or bi-weekly cadence. Playbooks and factories

Your second-order accelerants are reusable playbooks. Start with three:

1. **Discovery to Decision Pack:** The intake to Gate A artifacts from Chapter 12, templated.
2. **Prompting and Evaluation:** A repository (folder of reusable pieces) of prompt patterns, retrieval blueprints, and evaluation datasets and scripts.
3. **Guardrails as Code:** Policies turned into CI checks and runtime enforcement. If it cannot fail a build or block a release, when necessary, it is not yet a guardrail.

Create a simple internal catalog page that lists every playbook and tool, explains how to use each, and shows a single support contact for each. Give each playbook an owner and publish update notes.

Gates - Sequential by Domain

Gates are the formal checkpoints where you decide to continue, expand, or stop an AI project or program. They occur in sequence within a business area (the "domain," e.g., Customer Support or Accounts Payable) and keep outcomes, reliability, and cost on track.

These gates keep risk small and help compound learning. We demonstrate value and stability in one area before expanding to add more users or enter another area. This avoids pilot sprawl, protects customer experience and budget, and ensures the same kit (prompts, checks, guardrails) is reusable.

Here, we outline three gates: A decides the pilot, B expands within the same domain, and C opens a new one.

Gate A: Pilot decision

Use Chapter 12's decision pack exactly as-is. Gate A is a pass or fail based on that pack. Your only additional step is to copy the winning pilot metrics into the domain's one-page KPI, economics, and reliability sheet, so it is ready for Gate B.

Gate B: Expand in the same domain

Criteria to move from a contained pilot to a wider population inside the same domain include:

- **Outcome:** The KPI improvement is repeatable in a second cohort.
- **Unit economics:** Per-interaction, or per-artifact cost, is on a downward trend.

- **Reliability:** SLOs are met for two consecutive review windows, and failures stay within the error budget. If that limit is being used up too quickly or exceeded, pause or slow new releases until stability returns.
- **Governance:** The six checks from *Governance six-check verification* are green or have time-boxed exceptions with owners.

Gate C: Add a new domain

Criteria to expand into a second domain:

- **The reuse kit** from the anchor domain has been published and is used in a real-world change.
- **Operating model** decision rights are exercised at least twice, for example, when a release is gated for reliability and a policy is updated in response to an incident.
- **The readiness** ARA re-run shows that at least two dimensions have improved, or the sponsor has explicitly accepted the risks with dates.
- **Capacity:** The platform team and risk partner can absorb the load without pushing reliability below SLOs across live use cases.

Deliverable for all gates: A gate checklist you can print on one side of a piece of paper and take to the decision meeting. Decisions are time-boxed to 30 minutes. Yes or no. Conditional, yes, but only with named owners and dates.

Conclusion: What to do now

If the essentials for developing an agentic system are already in place, hold a 2-hour workshop to confirm Gate A for your pilot domain. Lock the success targets and the unit-cost goals. Name the pod and make roles explicit. Agree on a weekly and a monthly review rhythm. Begin the first two weeks of Path A right away.

If you are at a medium-readiness level, start the eight-week preparation plan. Publish a short checklist of data and governance fixes with a progress tracker (a simple chart showing "tasks remaining" each week) so everyone can track progress. Put the adoption plan in front of line managers now so training and incentives are ready before launch.

If you are in the early stages of developing your agentic AI, do not rush the timeline. Treat the six-month foundation as a structured build phase with clear milestones and ownership, as you would for a product launch. Pick your rails, meaning the basic platform and policy standards you will use. Choose one anchor domain that will run on those rails. Aim for a "prove-the-rails" pilot at month six, not a one-off demo.

In every case, bring your finance partner into the monthly executive review from day one and link spend to the KPI tree and the unit-economics trend. This keeps decisions fast, keeps budgets tied to outcomes, and sets up the next quarter to scale with fewer surprises.

Scale is not what happens after you get lucky once. Scale is the operating model, the cadence, and the gates that keep you honest. Run governance and safety checks, manage error logs and budgets, track and publish performance updates, and let the reuse compounding do its quiet work.

References:

- McKinsey. "The state of AI in 2024."
- McKinsey. "Gen AI's next inflection point: from employee experimentation to organizational transformation." Operating-model requirements for sustained impact.
- McKinsey. "From promising to productive: real results from gen AI in services." Scaling evidence in operations and finance.
- AI TRiSM | Gartner
- IBM Think. "What is AI TRiSM?"
- The Next Generation Operating Model for the Digital World | McKinsey
- Organizing for digital acceleration: Making a two-speed IT operating model work | McKinsey
- The Digital Operating Model: Building a Componentized Organization | MIT CISR
- AI Center of Excellence | Deloitte US
- Impact Effort Matrix | What It Is and How to Use It Effectively? | Creately
- Responsible AI | The 2024 AI Index Report | Stanford HAI
- Foundations for scalable enterprise AI | IBM Think
- Gen-AI KPIs: measuring your AI success | Google Cloud
- Embracing risk and error budgets | Google SRE

CHAPTER 14

The Future of Agentic Systems

Executives are often skeptical when IT presents new cutting-edge technologies, such as agentic AI, to them. This is a good instinct. The road ahead for agentic systems is promising, crowded, and often overhyped. The practical view is that agents are transitioning from single prompts to outcome-driven actors that plan, utilize tools, learn from feedback, and operate under policy. The shape of that progress is already visible in research, in platform roadmaps, and in the patterns that worked in your pilots.

Two signals matter most for planning.

First, research and market trackers show steady productivity gains from AI programs that reach production with well-designed platforms and governance. McKinsey's 2025 work on enterprise AI describes how leaders create value by investing in platform capabilities, outcome measurement, and risk management, rather than relying on isolated models and demos.

Second, analysts expect adoption to shift toward agentic use cases that deliver narrow outcomes with clear service levels and controlled autonomy, rather than the free-form "AI everywhere" approach.

What follows is the argument in one line: capabilities are improving, constraints are not going away, so the only sensible way to move forward is to treat agentic AI like a portfolio and to give autonomy only to what you can test.

This chapter outlines a practical tour of near-term advances, the constraints that will still be relevant, and how to make informed bets.

What is Actually Getting Better

Three capability shifts are transitioning from the lab to the field.

1. **Self-evaluation and improvement:** Agents can critique their own outputs, write small tests, and iterate toward better answers. Research, such as Reflexion, shows that verbal feedback loops help language agents improve on reasoning tasks over multiple attempts. Self-Refine demonstrates similar effects by letting models revise drafts with their own feedback. Results vary by domain, but the direction is clear.

2. **Richer perception and action:** Vision-language-action research links what agents see to what they do. Google's RT-2 maps text and images directly to robot actions. AutoRT coordinates fleets of robots from natural-language tasks. For most enterprises, the exciting part is not a general-purpose robot. It is the concept of an agent that can actually operate a claims system or an internal app and follow rules within a constrained environment.

3. **Standardizing how agents use tools, store memory, and follow policy:** Model Context Protocol and orchestration libraries, such as AutoGen or LangGraph, aim to ensure that tool discovery, permissions, memory management, and tracing operate in a consistent manner. This is still early, but it points to a future where platform teams can give business teams a safe agent runtime instead of a basket of experiments.

What will Stay Difficult

A few constraints still persist..

Maintaining safe multi-tool workflows will continue to be a challenge. The more computer systems an agent touches, the more it will surprise you. Proving data lineage across agent memory is difficult. If an agent remembers something from a document last week, you must still be able to tell an auditor where that piece of knowledge came from. The cost for long chains of agents communicating with one another remains stubbornly high. Human-in-the-loop (HILP) agent output validation remains necessary for financial stability, customer satisfaction, and regulatory compliance.

None of these is a reason to stop your agentic program. They are simply reasons to design with each risk in mind from the first sprint (i.e., maintaining an engineering-minded discipline) instead of trying to add controls right before launch.

The Rule that Unlocks Everything

This is the most important sentence in the chapter:

No harness, no agent autonomy.

A harness is a method for verifying whether an agent performs as it was programmed. It can be real unit tests, synthetic tasks, golden examples, policy checks, or business rules. If you do not have that, you should not let the system act on its own. This is why agentic approaches have progressed more rapidly in code and document transformations than in open-ended marketing or cross-departmental workflows. Code and documents can be checked. Creative strategy cannot be checked cheaply.

Make it an organizational habit to ship agents only inside boxes that can be tested. Start by describing the outcome. Define what counts as a pass. Let the agent attempt the work and critique itself inside that box. Log everything. Once a harness is stable, expand the scope of what the agent is allowed to do. This is how you achieve genuine autonomy without surprises.

Agents That Write Their Own Tests

A useful way to think about "self-improvement" is to imagine an agent arriving with a small lab kit. It can propose tests, run them, and use the results to refine plans. Reflection and Self-Refine are early blueprints for that loop. The new class of code benchmarks makes the opportunity tangible. SWE-bench Verified evaluates whether a model can make multi-file changes that pass real unit tests in real repositories. That is closer to production work than simple Q&A.

Why this matters for business. If an agent can run a repeatable harness, it can improve without linear growth in human review. That does not remove oversight. It raises the floor on quality and accelerates iteration.

Where to use it first. Document transformations with clear acceptance checks. Code suggestions and small fixes. Structured operations where you can define "pass or fail" in a test harness.

Limits to expect. Gains are uneven in open-ended tasks. The loop still needs a ground-truth oracle. You must store evaluation traces along with the code so that you can replay and audit them. Otherwise, the "improvement" becomes an anecdote.

Where you will see agentic systems first

We can now examine the most promising areas through a harness lens.

Document-to-decision flows are a clear candidate. Contract review, intake classification, KYC steps, claim triage, and similar processes have a clear notion of correctness. You can let an agent read, extract, and reason at a narrow depth, and then pass to a human (HILP) for final approval. This provides speed, safety, and a clear audit trail.

Customer operations will follow closely behind. Give the agent permission to resolve Tier 1 issues, update records, and answer well-known questions. Keep escalation rules strict and simple. Since customer operations already have weekly and monthly reporting, you can demonstrate value quickly. Finance leaders understand this language.

Screen reading agents will move from labs to shadow mode. You can let an agent practice in a simulated web or OS environment, then run it in parallel with a real process without making final changes, and then graduate it to live action. Simulation is rehearsal. Shadow mode is probation - both lower risks.

Multi-agent orchestration will appear in processes that already resemble a relay race. An agent collects context, another retrieves it, another drafts it, another checks for policy, and a human signs off (HILP). These orchestrations can be highly productive if you limit the number of turns per outcome and measure the cost per completed task rather than tokens per model. Conversations between agents are charming, but they are not free.

Vision and embodied tasks will succeed first in controlled environments, such as inspection booths, micro-fulfillment, or retail shelf checks. Anywhere the scene is predictable and the cost of failure is low, you can let an agent perceive and act.

Standards for Tools, Memory, and Policy

Enterprises want agent systems that integrate seamlessly, adhere to established rules or industry best practices, and can be easily audited. That requires some shared language for tools, memory, and policy. The Model Context Protocol is an early attempt at establishing a standard for how agents discover tools and call them, with permissioning that can be mapped to enterprise roles. Expect a period of competing approaches. Also, expect the major platform providers to default to policy controls that enterprises already use, such as role-based access, data loss prevention hooks, key management, and structured audit logs.

Pragmatic posture: Prefer systems that expose tool manifests, permission scopes, and trace logs. Avoid heavy customization that locks you in. Standards are your friend even when they are young.

Governance That Lives in Code

Regulators are moving from discussion to enforcement. The EU AI Act imposes obligations for high-risk systems encompassing risk management, data governance, security, and post-deployment monitoring. Timelines begin phasing in before full applicability in 2026. In the United States, the NIST AI Risk Management Framework remains the practical reference for identifying, measuring, managing, and mitigating risks, as well as ensuring human oversight.

The direction is obvious. You must be able to show what an AI system did, under what policy, using what data, with what human involvement.

For agentic systems, this means that policy cannot reside solely in a Confluence page. It must reside in the code or a configuration file.

How to translate policy into controls:

- Implement allow-lists for tools and explicit scopes for data access.
- Treat agent memory like sensitive data. It should be purpose-bound and tagged so you can explain why an agent acted in a certain way.

- Maintain human-in-the-loop checkpoints on consequential actions.
- Monitor and alert on off-policy behavior.
- Keep replayable traces that connect inputs, tool calls, and outputs to specific policies and versions, allowing for accurate analysis and troubleshooting.

Here is a concise way to tell this story within the company. Agents compose actions at runtime. Since they can improvise within the tools you give them, the policy must be in a place they can see at runtime. That is why governance must be codified. Consider this the long-term cost of winning. Systems that cannot be audited will not be allowed to run.

What to Pilot, What to Bet Lightly, What to Park

You can express the whole adoption strategy through three verbs and three questions.

Pilots ask whether we can prove functionality this quarter. They are use cases with clear outcomes, clear checks, and motivated business owners. Document to decision, narrow customer operations, and sandboxed screen agents belong here.

Bet asks whether we can learn safely. These are use cases where the value is attractive, but the environment or orchestration is still changing. Vision tasks in a factory cell, or multi-agent processes for marketing that must remain brand-safe, fit here. You run them with limits.

Park asks whether we can avoid getting hurt. These are ideas that sound exciting but do not yet have a cheap way to be evaluated. Unbounded autonomy across departments, or open-ended generation without a reviewer, or anything that implies legal personhood or unreviewed financial authority, stays in R&D until it can be tested.

Once people learn this vocabulary, it becomes very easy to have portfolio conversations. A sales leader can say this is a pilot. A supply chain leader can say this is a limited bet. Risk can say this is parked until we have a harness. Everyone knows what that means.

Architecture Patterns That Will Stick

Outcome-first orchestration: Express the business goal as a task graph with quality gates, not a single prompt. Use nodes for retrieval, decision, and drafting; attach tests and rollback logic. LangGraph's approach is a good mental model.

Policy as code: Write policies that agents execute, not just documents on a wiki. Tool allow-lists, rate limits, escalation rules, and data retention should be managed in a configuration file with clear code version control. Map these to NIST RMF "govern, map, measure, manage" so audits are faster.

Memory with purpose binding: Partition short-term scratchpads from durable knowledge. Label sources. Apply retention windows. This reduces risk and helps you answer "why did it act that way" with an actual trace rather than a shrug.

Evaluation harnesses: Keep small but honest datasets and unit tests next to the code. If the agent claims to improve, it must pass its own tests.

Operating the System, Not Just the Model

As agents become products, the operating model changes.

- **From model-ops to agent-ops:** Teams manage prompts, tools, policies, memory, and traces in addition to models. They own cost control, reliability, and rollback.
- **Roles shift:** Business SMEs must curate risk and governance policies and address edge cases. Reviewers adjudicate exceptions. Platform teams provide observability and sandboxes.
- **Budgeting matures:** Move from token accounting to unit economics by outcome. Define a unit of value, such as a resolved ticket or processed claim. Tie vendor pricing to that unit where possible.

What Could Go Wrong and How to Hedge

Hallucinated actions: Prevent hallucinations with strict tool schemas, confirmation prompts for destructive steps, and post-action verification. Treat tool use like writing to a production database: never allow it to exist without guardrails in place.

Cost drift: Long, chatty chains can quickly burn a budget. Cap chain length. Use per-task budgets. Sample traces and score them for efficiency.

Policy drift: Prompts and tools change over time, so review both regularly. Set alerts to notify you when behavior deviates from company policy.

Over-automation: Don't remove humans from all parts of your automated processes. Instead, keep human review on high-impact decisions. Measure false positives, escalations, and time-to-recovery.

A Portfolio for the Next 12–24 Months

1. Anchor on two or three use cases with production-credible evaluation. Choose to move forward with use cases where simulation or shadow mode can quickly prove safety and value.
2. Build a small "agent platform core." Orchestration, memory, policy, observability, and sandboxes are necessary and reliable parts of any pilot or production program.
3. Focus attention on emerging agentic standards. Watch MCP and similar related programs for tool discovery, permissioning, and tracing standards. Utilize industry best practice standards to minimize integration costs.
4. Publish a line-of-business intake form. Request the outcomes, guardrails, data sources, and success metrics needed to evidence success from a pilot.
5. Measure your pilot or production programs using business metrics first, model metrics second. Track the value stream and the risk stream. Report both.

A Realistic Picture of "Good" in 2026

A mature enterprise will run a handful of certified autonomous workflows. Each has clear service levels, policy-as-code controls, and full traceability. Most other flows use human-in-the-loop patterns with narrow autonomy and reliable handoff. Platform teams provide shared sandboxes, tool catalogs, memory services, and audit trails. Quarterly reports should demonstrate value in terms of claims processed, tickets resolved, or improved customer experience, not just model calls. Audits will be passed because everything was logged, not because everyone was lucky.

It will look less like a sci-fi company and more like a very competent operations team that happens to have clever agents.

Conclusion: The Strange, Useful Future

Agent capabilities are widening. Agents can plan, critique their own work, utilize tools, view computer screens, and coordinate with other agents. At the same time, old but necessary enterprise constraints remain unchanged. You still need to demonstrate the origin of the data, maintain control over costs, ensure human approval for sensitive actions, and retain the ability to replay what happened. Because the two lines move at different speeds, the winning pattern is always the same: define an outcome, put the rules in code, test honestly, then increase autonomy.

It is fine to keep a sense of wonderment when creating agentic systems. Systems that write small tests for themselves and learn from those results feel strange. Robots that can follow natural-language instructions to do simple tasks feel stranger. Simulated worlds where agents practice for weeks before they touch production are cooler than most slides can capture.

Keep a sense of wonderment, but pair it with discipline, and add a dash of skepticism to everything that is happening. The future of agentic AI will reward teams that can hold those things at once.

The horizon ahead is not magic. It is a patient compounding of well-thought-through decisions. If you build agentic AI workflows for business outcomes, encode policy in code, and insist on rigorous evaluation at each step. You should be able to trust the agents you build will be more than clever demos. They will be colleagues who work side by side with your human workforce, take direction, and help your organization move with agility and care simultaneously.

References

- Rewarding AI transformations: How leaders invest and design for impact
- Top Strategic Predictions for 2025 and Beyond | Gartner
- Reflection: "Language Agents with Verbal Reinforcement Learning."
- Self-Refine: "Iterative Feedback from Models for Text Generation."
- SWE-bench Verified benchmark
- RT-2 vision-language-action explained
- Google AutoRT robot fleet coordination
- Open-X Embodiment project
- MineDojo
- Habitat by Meta AI
- NVIDIA Isaac Sim
- WebArena web environment
- OSWorld computer-use benchmark
- Microsoft AutoGen
- LangGraph
- Anthropic Model Context Protocol
- EU AI Act explainer and legal text access
- NIST AI Risk Management Framework

APPENDIX A

The Agentic Readiness Assessment (ARA) Worksheet

Purpose

This worksheet provides a structured framework for assessing your organization's readiness to successfully implement and scale an agentic AI initiative. Its purpose is to establish an honest, evidence-based baseline of your current capabilities and identify critical bottlenecks before you commit significant resources.

Treat this not as a test to be passed, but as a diagnostic tool to guide your strategic planning. An honest assessment is the first step toward a successful implementation.

Instructions

1. **Assemble a Cross-Functional Team:** The assessment should be completed by a small group representing key functions: a business owner (who feels the pain point), a technical lead (from data or engineering), and a representative from risk, legal, or governance.
2. **Review Each Dimension:** Discuss each of the six dimensions below as a team.
3. **Assign a Score (0–5):** Based on the scoring rubric, assign a score that reflects your organization's *current state*, not its future ambition.
4. **Provide Evidence:** For each score, you must cite specific evidence or examples in the "Evidence/Notes" column. This is the most critical step to avoid opinion-based scoring.
5. **Summarize and Plan:** Complete the summary section to identify your top three bottlenecks and create an initial remediation plan with clear ownership and timelines.

Agentic Readiness Assessment

Dimension	Score (0–5)	Evidence / Notes (Provide specific examples, documents, or systems)
1. Business Clarity		
2. Data Readiness		
3. Architecture & Platform		
4. People & Skills		
5. Governance & Risk		
6. Change & Adoption		

Scoring Rubric

Dimension	Low Score (0–1)	Medium Score (2–3)	High Score (4–5)
1. Business Clarity	AI goals are vague ("explore AI"). No clear P&L link or accountable executive. Success is measured by activity, not business outcomes.	A specific use case is identified. An executive sponsor is named, but success KPIs are not yet defined or baselined. Ownership is informal.	AI program outcomes are explicitly tied to P&L or mission goals. Every use case has a single, accountable executive. KPIs are baselined, and targets are signed off.
2. Data Readiness	Critical data is siloed, of poor quality, or only accessible through manual reports. No clear data governance or access policies for AI use.	Data is identified, but access requires significant manual effort or new engineering work. Data quality is inconsistent. Policies exist but are not consistently enforced.	Key data is accessible via policy-compliant APIs with acceptable quality and latency. Data lineage is documented for critical sources. Governance is clear and auditable.
3. Architecture & Platform	No shared platform exists. Every project is a custom build. No central services for security, monitoring, or model access.	Some reusable components exist but are not standardized. Observability is manual and reactive. The production environment is not fully hardened for AI workloads.	A secure, production-grade runtime exists with centralized observability, model access, and reliable integrations. A platform team provides shared, stable services.
4. People & Skills	No dedicated team. Work is done by individuals on a "side-of-desk" basis. Roles and responsibilities are unclear. Lack of in-house agent engineering or integration skills.	A team is assigned, but members are part-time and split across other priorities. Some technical skills exist, but key roles like Product Owner or SME are not formally defined.	Cross-functional pods are staffed with dedicated time. Roles (Product Owner, SME, Agent Engineer) are clearly defined. A plan for upskilling or hiring is in place.

5. Governance & Risk	No formal policies for AI. Risk management is ad-hoc and reactive. No model inventory, bias testing, or incident response plan exists.	Policies are documented in wikis but not implemented in code. Controls are manual and applied inconsistently. Risk is discussed but not formally measured.	Policies are implemented as automated controls ("policy-as-code"). A model inventory is maintained. Bias testing, monitoring, and incident response plans are in place and tested.
6. Change & Adoption	No plan for user training or adoption. The project is seen as a "tech-only" initiative. Line managers are not engaged or aware of the project.	A communication plan exists, but there is no formal training program. Some managers are engaged, but there is no network of champions to drive adoption.	Line managers are actively engaged. A formal adoption plan with training is in place. Champions have been identified and empowered. Telemetry is set up to track user adoption.

Assessment Summary & Action Plan

1. Readiness Heat Map

(Color-code each box based on the score: Red for 0–1, Yellow for 2–3, Green for 4–5)

Dimension	**Score**	**Rating**
Business Clarity		
Data Readiness		
Architecture & Platform		
People & Skills		
Governance & Risk		
Change & Adoption		
Overall Readiness:		*(Avg. Score)*

2. Top 3 Bottlenecks

(Based on your lowest and most critical scores, what are the three biggest blockers to success?)

1.

2.

3.

3. Remediation Plan

(Turn your findings into an action plan. This will become the first input into your program roadmap.)

Bottleneck Identified	Action Required to Remediate	Owner	Target Date
1.			
2.			
3.			

B APPENDIX

One-Page Business Case Template

Agentic AI Business Case: [Project Name]

Date:	[Date]	**Executive Sponsor:**	[Sponsor's Name]
Version:	1.0	**Business Owner:**	[Owner's Name]

The Proposal: We request a total Year 1 investment of **$[Total Year 1 Investment]** to deploy the **[Project Name]**, an agentic AI system to **[State the primary business outcome]**. Based on conservative projections, this initiative is expected to deliver a **[Projected ROI %]** return on investment and achieve payback within **[Payback Period in Months]** months.

The "Before" Story: The Problem	The "After" Story: The Solution
Currently, **[Describe the business process]** is a significant bottleneck... **Cost:** Costing **$[Annual Cost]** annually... **Speed:** Average cycle time is **[Number]** days/hours... **Risk:** The manual process has an error rate of **[Error Rate %]**.	We will deploy an AI agent to **[Describe the new, automated workflow]**... **Outcome:** This will improve **[Metric]** by **[Improvement %]**... **Strategic Alignment:** This project directly supports our corporate goal to **[State Goal]**.

The Investment (Year 1)	**The Return (Conservative Case Projection - Annual)**
One-Time Costs **Development & Integration: $[Amount]** **Total One-Time: $[Amount]** **Recurring Costs** **Platform & Infrastructure: $[Amount]** **Total Recurring: $[Amount]** **Total Year 1 Investment: $[Amount]**	**1. Efficiency Gains:** $[Amount] **2. Revenue Generation:** $[Amount] **3. Risk Mitigation:** $[Amount] **4. Business Agility:** *Strategic Value* **Total Projected Annual Return: $[Amount]**

Financial Summary	**Implementation Timeline & Milestones**
Total Year 1 Investment: $[Amount] **Projected Annual Return: [Amount]** **Projected Year 1 ROI: [ROI %]** **Conservative Payback Period: [Number] Months**	**Phase 1 (Weeks 1-4): Pilot Program ↓** **Phase 2 (Weeks 5-12): Scaled Rollout ↓** **Phase 3 (Week 13+): Value Realization**

Appendix C

AI Pilot Program Charter Template

Purpose and Instructions

A successful pilot is not an experiment; it is a disciplined, time-boxed project designed to produce decision-grade evidence. This charter serves as the single source of truth for the 4-week pilot program described in Chapter 12. Its purpose is to ensure absolute alignment on goals, scope, and success criteria among all stakeholders *before* the first line of code is written.

Complete this document with your pilot team and secure formal sign-off from the Executive Sponsor. This charter is your primary defense against the common causes of pilot failure: unclear scope, undefined metrics, and mismatched expectations.

AI Pilot Program Charter: [Project Name]

Project Name:	[e.g., Customer Support Email Triage Agent]	**Date:**
Executive Sponsor:	[Sponsor's Name, Title]	**Business Owner:**
Project Lead:	[Lead's Name, Title]	**Pilot Duration:**

1. Pilot Objective & Value Hypothesis

(Describe the business outcome you are trying to achieve in a single, clear paragraph. Reference Chapter 12 for the value hypothesis format.)

Within four weeks, this agentic pilot will [Action, e.g., reduce average response time for Tier-1 support tickets] from [Baseline Metric, e.g., 24 hours] to [Target Metric, e.g., 4 hours] for the pilot user group. This will validate the business case that agentic AI can [Broader Business Goal, e.g., improve customer satisfaction and reduce operational costs].

2. Measurable Success Criteria (KPIs)

(This is the pilot's scorecard. The pilot is successful only if it meets these pre-defined targets.)

KPI	Baseline (Current)	Target (End of Pilot)	Measurement Method
1. [Primary Metric, e.g., Avg. Resolution Time]	[e.g., 48 hours]	[e.g., < 12 hours]	[e.g., Zendesk Reporting]
2. [Secondary Metric, e.g., User Satisfaction]	[e.g., 3.8 / 5.0]	[e.g., > 4.2 / 5.0]	[e.g., Post-interaction survey]
3. [Operational Metric, e.g., Cost per Interaction]	[e.g., $12.50]	[e.g., < $9.00]	[e.g., Cost telemetry + ticket volume]
4. [Technical Metric, e.g., Agent Accuracy]	N/A	[e.g., > 90%]	[e.g., Manual audit of 100 random cases]

3. Scope

(Be ruthless in defining a minimalist scope. The goal is to prove the value hypothesis, not build a feature-complete system.)

In-Scope	Out-of-Scope (Deferred until after successful pilot)
The single workflow of [e.g., triaging inbound emails].	Integration with [e.g., the knowledge base].
Integration with [e.g., Zendesk and Salesforce (read-only)].	A user-facing interface or dashboard.
Handling the [e.g., "Billing" and "Technical Support"] intents.	Handling non-English language inquiries.
A pilot group of [e.g., 5 users from the Tier-1 team].	Any feature not essential to moving the KPIs above.

4. Pilot Timeline & Key Milestones

- **Week 1:** Discovery & Design: Finalize scope, KPIs, and thin-slice architecture. Confirm data access. (Milestone: Signed Charter)
- **Week 2: Core Development:** Build the primary agent workflow with production-grade logging and monitoring. (Milestone: Working Demo of Core Path)
- **Week 3:** Integration & Testing: Complete system integrations and run structured User Acceptance Testing (UAT). (Milestone: UAT Complete)
- **Week 4:** Deployment & Measurement: Deploy to the pilot user group and measure performance against KPIs. (Milestone: Go/No-Go Decision Pack Presented)

5. Key Stakeholders & Roles

Role	Name	Responsibilities
Executive Sponsor		Secure budget, remove organizational blockers, make the final Go/No-Go decision.
Business Owner		Owns the business outcome, validates KPIs, drives user adoption.
Project Lead		Manages the pilot plan, facilitates daily standups, reports progress.
Technical Lead		Owns the agent architecture and ensures production readiness.
Subject Matter Expert(s)		Provide process knowledge, participate in testing, validate agent outputs.

6. Risks & Assumptions

Risk/Assumption	Impact	Mitigation Plan
Risk: Data access delays	High	Confirm all required API keys and permissions in Week 1.
Risk: Scope creep	High	The "Out-of-Scope" list is enforced by the Project Lead in every review.
Assumption: Partner knowledge transfer	Medium	Contractually require daily pairing sessions and weekly architecture walkthroughs.

APPENDIX D

Sample Job Descriptions for Key Agentic Roles

Purpose and Instructions

The arrival of agentic AI creates new, business-critical roles that bridge technology and strategy. As outlined in Chapter 3, these roles are essential for building a successful human-AI team. Use these templates as a starting point for your recruiting efforts. Adapt the specifics to fit your industry and company culture. (Note: Salary bands mentioned in Chapter 3 are for planning purposes and typically not included in public job descriptions.)

Job Description: AI Agent Orchestrator

Position Title: AI Agent Orchestrator
Department: [e.g., Business Operations, Customer Success, AI Center of Excellence]
Reports To: [e.g., Director of Operations]

Role Summary:

The AI Agent Orchestrator acts as the "manager" of our digital workforce. This role is responsible for overseeing the performance, quality, and workflow integration of our AI agents to ensure they are achieving their intended business outcomes. You will not be coding the agents, but you will be the strategic mind directing their efforts, optimizing their processes, and ensuring seamless collaboration between our human and AI team members.

Core Responsibilities:

- **Performance Management:** Monitor a portfolio of AI agents against their defined business KPIs (e.g., efficiency, accuracy, cost-per-transaction).
- **Workflow Optimization:** Analyze agent decision logs and performance data to identify bottlenecks, improve routing logic, and enhance agent effectiveness.
- **Quality Assurance:** Establish and maintain quality standards for agent outputs, conducting regular audits and creating feedback loops for continuous improvement.
- **Human-in-the-Loop Management:** Design and manage the escalation pathways from AI agents to human experts, ensuring a smooth and efficient handoff process.
- **Stakeholder Collaboration:** Act as the primary liaison between the business units using the agents and the technical teams building them, translating business needs into agent behavior requirements.

Required Skills & Qualifications:

- 5+ years of experience in business operations, process improvement, or project management.
- Strong analytical skills with a demonstrated ability to use data to drive decisions.
- Excellent understanding of business process mapping and workflow design.
- Exceptional communication skills, with the ability to explain complex systems to non-technical stakeholders.
- A strategic mindset with a focus on achieving measurable business outcomes.
- *Preferred:* Experience working with automation platforms, business intelligence tools, or in a role overseeing operational systems.

Job Description: Prompt Engineer / AI Interaction Designer

Position Title: Prompt Engineer / AI Interaction Designer
Department: [e.g., Product, Marketing, AI Center of Excellence]
Reports To: [e.g., Head of Product, AI Orchestration Lead]

Role Summary:

The AI Interaction Designer is the "communications expert" who shapes how our AI agents think, behave, and communicate. You will craft the core instructions, guardrails, and persona that define our agents' interactions with customers. This role is a unique blend of technical writing, user experience design, and business strategy, ensuring our agents are not only effective but also on-brand, reliable, and trustworthy.

Core Responsibilities:

- **Instruction Architecture:** Design, write, and maintain the master prompts and instruction sets that govern agent behavior for various business workflows.
- **Agent Persona & Voice:** Develop and enforce a consistent brand voice, tone, and persona for all customer-facing and internal AI agents.
- **Testing & Validation:** Create and manage a library of test cases (including adversarial tests) to systematically evaluate agent performance, identify failure modes, and ensure reliability.

- **Quality Optimization:** Analyze agent responses and user feedback to continuously refine and improve prompts for better accuracy, clarity, and goal achievement.
- **Documentation & Best Practices:** Codify and share best practices for effective prompt engineering across the organization, building a reusable library of high-performing prompt patterns.

Required Skills & Qualifications:

- 3+ years of experience in a role requiring precise and structured communication, such as technical writing, UX writing, copywriting, or instructional design.
- A deep curiosity and intuitive understanding of how Large Language Models (LLMs) interpret language.
- A highly logical and structured thinking process, with the ability to break down complex processes into clear, unambiguous instructions.
- Experience with systematic testing and quality assurance methodologies.
- Strong ability to collaborate with both technical and non-technical teams.
- *Preferred:* Direct experience writing prompts for generative AI platforms (e.g., for chatbots, content generation, or other LLM-powered applications).

Job Description: AI Ethics & Compliance Officer

Position Title: AI Ethics & Compliance Officer
Department: [e.g., Legal, Risk & Compliance, AI Center of Excellence]
Reports To: [e.g., Chief Risk Officer, General Counsel]

Role Summary:

The AI Ethics & Compliance Officer serves as the "conscience and shield" of our AI operations, ensuring that all agentic systems are deployed responsibly, ethically, and in full compliance with legal and regulatory standards. You will be responsible for proactively identifying and mitigating the unique risks associated with autonomous systems, including data privacy and bias, brand safety, and regulatory adherence.

Core Responsibilities:

- **AI Governance Framework:** Develop, implement, and manage an enterprise-wide governance framework for agentic AI, aligning with standards such as the NIST AI Risk Management Framework and regulations like the EU AI Act.

- **Risk Assessment:** Conduct formal risk assessments for all new AI agent deployments, evaluating potential impacts on customers, the business, and the brand.
- **Bias Detection & Mitigation:** Lead initiatives to test for and mitigate algorithmic bias in agent decision-making, ensuring fair and equitable outcomes.
- **Regulatory Compliance:** Act as the subject matter expert on AI-related regulations, ensuring our agent deployments meet all legal requirements in the jurisdictions where we operate.
- **Incident Response:** In partnership with security and operations, manage responses to any ethical or compliance incidents related to AI agent behavior, conducting root cause analyses and implementing corrective actions.

Required Skills & Qualifications:

- 5+ years of experience in a risk management, legal, compliance, or public policy role, preferably within a technology or highly regulated industry.
- Deep understanding of risk management frameworks and principles.
- Familiarity with the ethical challenges of AI, including bias, fairness, and transparency.
- Strong analytical skills and the ability to translate complex regulatory requirements into practical operational controls.
- Excellent judgment and the ability to provide clear, pragmatic guidance to business and technical teams.
- *Preferred:* A law degree (J.D.) or a background in technology policy. Direct experience with AI-specific regulations (e.g., EU AI Act).

GLOSSARY OF TERMS

Agentic AI (aka Agentic AI) - Agentic AI, also known as 'agents' or 'autonomous agents', refers to autonomous AI systems that can make decisions and perform actions with minimal human intervention. These agents can understand their environment, identifying the set of tools and functions at their disposal, and using those to take actions to achieve their objectives.

Agent-based systems - use Foundation Models (primarily Large Language Models, or LLMs) to align their capabilities with their objectives. For example, an order processing system may have multiple agents autonomously capturing pricing and market-related data. When a request for an order is raised, the agentic system may use those prices or, if they haven't been updated recently, may use another agent to retrieve the latest available price. This all happens automatically in the background because the system knows which agents are capable of performing each task.

These systems offer a simpler approach to building powerful AI-driven solutions by focusing on the capabilities of each agent and allowing the AI model to determine the best way to achieve the system's objectives. The high level of abstraction involved in this technology makes it easier to create more efficient and effective systems that take full advantage of AI.

Agent Loop (Perceive, Think, Act, Learn) - The continuous, four-stage operational cycle that defines a true **Agentic AI** system. The agent **(1) Perceives** data from its environment, **(2) Thinks** by reasoning and planning, **(3) Acts** by executing tasks via **Tools**, and **(4) Learns** by observing outcomes to improve future performance.

Agent Memory - The capability of an AI agent to retain and recall information across interactions. This includes short-term "working memory" for conversational context and long-term "institutional memory" powered by technologies like **Retrieval-Augmented Generation (RAG)** and **Vector Databases**.

Agent Orchestrator - The role (often human) or system (a "coordinator agent") responsible for managing a workforce of AI agents. Like an orchestra conductor, the orchestrator sets objectives, monitors performance, optimizes workflows, and ensures the agents are aligned with broader business goals.

Agent Swarm - A multi-agent system where a collection of specialized agents collaborate to solve complex problems that are beyond the capability of any single agent. A "coordinator" agent often directs the swarm, assigning tasks to specialists in areas like research, data analysis, or customer communication.

API (Application Programming Interface) - APIs are the "hands" of an AI agent. They are the mechanism through which an agent performs **Tool Use**—connecting to your CRM, ERP, or other business systems to read data and take action. A strong API strategy is a prerequisite for effective agent deployment.

Architecture - The foundational design or blueprint of an AI system. It defines how components, such as **Foundation Models**, data pipelines, security controls, and integrations, fit together. Key architectural decisions involve trade-offs between approaches, such as **Serverless** vs. **Containers**.

Artificial Intelligence (AI) - Artificial Intelligence is the development of computer software to perform tasks normally requiring human intelligence, such as visual perception, speech recognition, decision-making, and translation between languages. AI is not new. The term 'artificial intelligence' was coined in 1956 during the Dartmouth workshop, a gathering of scientists intent on exploring the potential of computing to emulate human reasoning. Since then, there have been recurring waves of progress and excitement, known as 'AI summers,' followed by periods of waning interest and investment, referred to as 'AI winters.'

Artificial General Intelligence (AGI) - Artificial General Intelligence refers to highly autonomous systems that possess the ability to understand, learn, and apply intelligence across a wide range of tasks at a human-like level. Unlike narrow AI, which is designed for specific tasks such as image recognition or language translation, AGI can reason, adapt, and perform any intellectual task that a human can. The concept of AGI has been a long-standing goal in AI research, with origins dating back to the early discussions of machine intelligence. While considerable progress has been made in artificial intelligence, AGI remains largely theoretical, with ongoing debates about its feasibility, potential impact, and ethical implications.

BIAS - A systematic prejudice in an AI model's outputs, leading to unfair or discriminatory outcomes. Bias often originates from skewed or unrepresentative training data that reflects historical or social inequities. AI-augmented sentencing software has been found to recommend higher prison sentences for Black offenders compared to white ones, even for equal crimes. And some facial recognition software works better for white faces than black ones.

Build vs. Buy Decision - The strategic choice an organization makes between developing a custom AI solution in-house (**Build**) or purchasing a solution or implementation services from a third-party vendor (**Buy**).

Centre of Expertise - A central team that functions as the "hub" in an agentic organization's "hub-and-spoke" model. The CoE is responsible for the strategic AI roadmap, developing reusable agent capabilities, and establishing enterprise-wide **Governance** and risk management standards.

Chain-of-thought (CoT) - A prompting technique that instructs a Large Language Model (LLM) to "think step-by-step," breaking down a complex problem into a sequence of intermediate reasoning steps. This significantly improves the accuracy of its final answer. This approach mimics human reasoning processes, allowing AI models to "think out loud" and articulate their thought process step-by-step before arriving at a final answer. It is a foundational technique for agentic reasoning patterns, such as **ReAct**.

Change Management - A structured approach for ensuring that changes to an organization are implemented smoothly and successfully to achieve lasting benefits. For AI adoption, this involves communicating the "why," empowering champions, and investing in systematic training. A deliberate change management strategy is the single biggest predictor of whether an AI initiative will succeed and scale or fail to gain adoption.

Chatbots - A reactive software application designed to simulate a simple, single-turn conversation based on pre-programmed scripts or a limited knowledge base. In more advanced versions, artificial intelligence (AI) techniques like natural language processing (NLP) are used to understand and respond to user inputs in a natural, conversational manner. They can be used for various purposes, including customer service, information gathering, and entertainment.

Code-First vs. Low-Code - Two primary approaches to building agentic systems. **Code-First** (e.g., using **Python** and **LangChain**) offers maximum control, customization, and scalability but requires specialized technical skills. **Low-Code** (e.g., using visual workflow builders) prioritizes speed and accessibility for non-technical users but offers less flexibility.

Compounding Advantage - A strategic benefit that grows at an accelerating rate over time. In the context of AI, early adopters gain a compounding advantage because their agents begin learning from real-world interactions on day one. The data, operational expertise, and customer insights generated by an agent do not grow linearly but compound, making it exponentially harder for competitors who wait to catch up. This is the core argument for the urgency of adopting agentic AI now.

Computer Vision (CV) - is a field of AI and machine learning that enables computers to interpret, analyze, and understand visual information (images and videos) to perform tasks such as object recognition, facial recognition, and scene understanding. Computer Vision systems are designed to make image data understandable and interpretable, allowing it to be consumed and evaluated. CV uses algorithms to break down images into pixels and process the pixels to detect edges, shapes, and colors. The system then uses this information to recognize objects, people, or scenes – similarly to how our brains process visual information – allowing computers to identify the content of images.

Containers - are a standardized unit of software that packages up code and all its dependencies so the application runs quickly and reliably from one computing environment to another. **Kubernetes** is the most common system for managing containers.

CRM (Customer Relationship Management) - A technology system for managing all of a company's relationships and interactions with current and potential customers. A CRM helps centralize customer data, track communication history, and manage sales pipelines. For an AI agent, the CRM is a primary source of customer context and a key system for taking action. Agents use the CRM as a **Tool** to look up a customer's history, value, and recent interactions and to execute tasks like creating new sales leads or updating contact records.

Data pipelines - A series of automated steps that move raw data from various sources to a destination (like a data warehouse or a **Vector Database**), transforming it along the way to make it clean, structured, and ready for use. Data pipelines are the essential plumbing required to give your agent a reliable **Memory**. They are responsible for continuously feeding and updating the knowledge base for a **RAG** system, ensuring the agent's responses are based on fresh, accurate, and relevant information. A failure in the data pipeline means the agent is working with stale data, which is a major operational risk.

DevOps - is the set of practices, tools, and a cultural philosophy that combine software development (Dev) and IT operations (Ops) to shorten the development life cycle and provide continuous delivery with high software quality. A mature DevOps culture is essential for deploying and maintaining production-grade AI agents, ensuring reliability, maintainability, and security.

ERP (Enterprise Resource Planning) - A type of software that organizations use to manage day-to-day business activities such as accounting, procurement, project management, risk management and compliance, and supply chain operations. Agents connect to ERPs via **APIs** to automate core business workflows that go beyond customer-facing tasks, such as checking inventory levels, validating financial data, or initiating procurement processes.

EU AI Act - A comprehensive legal framework from the European Union that regulates AI systems based on their level of risk. It imposes strict obligations on "high-risk" systems related to risk management, data governance, and human oversight.

Event-Driven Messaging - A communication protocol where agents interact by publishing messages (events) to a central channel rather than communicating directly with each other. Other agents can "subscribe" to the events that are relevant to them. This is the communication backbone of a scalable **Agent**

Swarm. It decouples agents, allowing the system to handle a massive volume of interactions without creating bottlenecks, ensuring high performance and reliability.

Fine Tuning - The process of further training a pre-trained **Foundation Model** on a smaller, domain-specific dataset to specialize its capabilities. Fine-tuning instills deep "semantic memory" in an agent, making it an expert in a specific field (e.g., medical terminology or financial analysis). This is a more intensive process than **RAG** and is used when an agent needs to learn a specialized skill, not just access facts.

Foundation Models - are large-scale, general-purpose artificial intelligence models that serve as the underlying architecture for a variety of more specialized applications. Models, such as GPT-4, are trained on vast datasets and are capable of understanding and generating human-like text, making them highly versatile for various AI tasks. Their size and complexity mean that they require significant computational resources to train and are usually only available to large organizations.

Generative AI - is the field of artificial intelligence that focuses on creating new content based on existing data. It is a subset of AI capable of generating text, images, audio, video, or other forms of output by using probabilistic models trained across various domains. Generative AI learns from vast amounts of carefully curated training data to identify and replicate complex patterns and structures. The output of generative AI models mimics the characteristics learned from the training data, enabling a range of novel applications. These include personalized content generation, advanced analysis and evaluation, and aiding creative processes. For a ChatBot or CRM system, generative AI can be used to create a range of helpful outputs, from writing personalized marketing content to generating synthetic data to test new features or strategies.

Examples of publicly accessible generative AI tools are ChatGPT, Claude, Gemini, and Dall-E. Generative AI is also becoming increasingly integrated into mainstream products. Examples include the Adobe Photoshop Generative Fill tool, AWS ChatOps Chatbot, Microsoft 365 Copilot, and Google Duet AI.

Governance - The comprehensive framework of policies, processes, roles, and controls that direct and manage an organization's AI initiatives. It covers everything from risk management and compliance to data quality and ethical oversight.

Guardrails - Automated safety controls designed to prevent an AI agent from producing harmful, off-brand, or unsafe outputs. They can be thought of as highway barriers that prevent catastrophic outcomes.

Hallucination - is a significant shortcoming in large language models (LLMs) and their derivative chatbots, characterized by their propensity to generate false information. Tools like Microsoft's Bing, Google's Gemini, or ChatGPT, for instance, have been known to fabricate non-existent articles as references to make confident but incorrect statements.

Human In The Loop (HILP) - is a workflow design pattern where an AI agent must pause and request human review, approval, or intervention before performing a high-stakes or irreversible action (e.g., transferring funds, deleting customer data).

Hybrid Search - A sophisticated information retrieval technique that combines semantic (or vector) search with traditional keyword-based search. This approach ensures that searches capture both the contextual meaning of a query and any specific, critical keywords (like product names or acronyms).

Hybrid Workforce - A team structure where human employees and AI agents collaborate to achieve business outcomes. In this model, humans typically focus on strategy, creative problem-solving, and relationship management, while agents handle data analysis, task execution, and process automation.

Knowledge Agent - An evolution of a workflow agent that is equipped with long-term **Memory** through **Retrieval-Augmented Generation (RAG)**. It can access and reason over an organization's entire body of institutional knowledge (documents, databases, past support cases) to provide contextually rich, expert-level answers and guidance.

KPI (Key Performance Indicator) - A quantifiable measure used to evaluate the success of an organization, team, or initiative in meeting its objectives. AI **pilot programs** must be tied to clear business KPIs (e.g., reduction in customer response time, increase in lead conversion rate) from day one. Measuring success with business metrics, not technical vanity metrics, is essential for proving value.

LangChain - is a popular open-source framework for building applications powered by LLMs. It provides standardized components to "chain" together prompts, LLM models, and tools.

LangGraph - is an extension of **LangChain** used to build more complex, stateful agent systems (like **Swarms**) where the workflow can include cycles and branches.

Large Language Models (LLMs) - are at the forefront of recent AI advancements. Notable examples include OpenAI's GPT-4 and Google's Gemini and Anthropic's Claude. These are massive artificial intelligence systems trained on extensive amounts of human language, primarily sourced from books and the internet.

They analyze and learn from the patterns of words in these datasets, becoming adept at mimicking human language.

Machine Learning (ML) - Machine Learning is considered a subset of artificial intelligence (AI). Machine learning uses computer algorithms to identify patterns within data. It is the branch of AI that learns from data. Those patterns are then used to create a data model that can make predictions. With increased data and experience, the results of machine learning become more accurate – much like how humans improve with more practice.

Microservices Architecture - A software development approach where a large application is built as a suite of small, independently deployable services. This is the standard architectural model for building scalable and resilient **Agent Swarms**. It allows different agent capabilities to be scaled, updated, and managed independently, preventing a failure in one agent from bringing down the entire system.

Neural networks - are a pivotal group of algorithms in machine learning, designed to emulate the structure of the human brain. They consist of nodes, like neurons in the brain, that perform calculations on data flowing through the connections between them. These networks are characterized by their inputs (such as training data) and outputs (like predictions or classifications).

NIST AI RMF - The AI Risk Management Framework from the U.S. National Institute of Standards and Technology. It provides a structured, voluntary framework for identifying, measuring, managing, and governing AI-related risks.

Observability - The ability to understand the internal state of an AI system from its external outputs. In practice, this means having detailed logs, traces, and metrics that allow you to answer "Why did the agent do that?"

OWASP Top 10 for LLMs - A standard awareness document from the Open Worldwide Application Security Project (OWASP) that identifies the ten most critical security risks for Large Language Model applications, including prompt injection and insecure tool use.

Pilot Program - A small-scale, controlled implementation of a new technology to prove its value and viability before a wider rollout.

Platform - In the context of agentic AI, a platform is a centralized and reusable set of foundational services, tools, and standards that accelerate the development, deployment, and management of multiple AI agents across an organization. A mature agent platform typically includes shared services for orchestration, **Memory** (e.g., vector databases), policy enforcement, **Observability**, security controls, and a catalog of pre-approved **Tools** and **APIs**.

Prompt Engineer - is the person responsible for crafting, testing, and refining the instructions (**Prompts**) given to AI agents. This role combines skills in technical writing, user experience design, and business process analysis to ensure agents behave reliably and align with brand voice.

Prompt engineering - is a process in the field of artificial intelligence (AI) and natural language processing (NLP) where careful design and formulation of input queries or prompts are used to elicit desired responses from AI models. It involves crafting the instructions or questions provided to the AI system in a way that maximizes the likelihood of obtaining accurate and relevant outputs.

Prototype - An early, experimental version of an AI agent built to test a concept or prove technical feasibility. It is distinct from a production-ready system, which is built with full **Architecture**, security, and reliability.

RAG - Retrieval-augmented generation (RAG) is a technique for refining generative AI models' precision, accuracy, and dependability by integrating information sourced from authoritative repositories. To grasp its essence, envision RAG as a legal researcher, gathering crucial facts and information from trusted legal repositories to enhance the accuracy and reliability of generative AI models, much like how a legal researcher strengthens the legal case strategy with solid legal foundations.

Reason-and-Act (ReAct) - is a core reasoning framework for agents that mimics human problem-solving. The agent cycles through three steps: 1) **Reason** about the current situation and plan the next action, 2) **Act** by using a tool, and 3) **Observe** the result to inform the next reasoning cycle.

Red Teaming - is the practice of adversarially testing an AI system to proactively identify vulnerabilities, biases, and potential failure modes. A "red team" acts like a sophisticated user trying to "break" the agent by using creative prompts to bypass its guardrails.

Return on Investment (ROI) - A performance metric used to evaluate the financial success of an AI investment. The book proposes a four-pillar framework for calculating ROI: Efficiency Gains, Revenue Generation, Risk Mitigation, and Business Agility.

Scalability - The ability of a system to handle a growing amount of work by adding resources. For an agentic system, this means it can handle increases in users, tasks, or data volume without a degradation in performance or a runaway increase in costs.

Serverless - A cloud computing model where the cloud provider manages the server infrastructure, and the user pays only for the compute time they consume.

For AI architecture, serverless ("a courier service") is ideal for event-driven, spiky workloads, as it minimizes idle costs and allows for rapid scaling. This contrasts with the higher-control model of **Containers**.

State Management - is the process of tracking and maintaining the current context, history, and status of a task or **Workflow** as it progresses. Robust state management is a technical prerequisite for reliable agentic workflows. It ensures that if one step fails, the agent can recover gracefully or escalate appropriately without losing the context of the entire process, which is critical for a positive customer experience.

Tool Chaining - A technique where an agent executes a sequence of **Tool Use** actions in a specific order, with the output from one tool becoming the input for the next. Tool chaining is the practical mechanism that enables agents to manage complex **Workflows**. It's how an agent can query a **CRM**, then check an **ERP**, and finally send a customer communication, with each step intelligently informing the next.

Tool Use - The ability of an AI agent to interact with and control other software or systems via **APIs**. This allows an agent to go beyond just generating text and take meaningful actions in the business world, such as searching a database, sending an email, or creating a calendar event. An agent that cannot use tools is simply a thinker without hands.

Vector Databases - A specialized type of database designed to store and search vector embeddings—numerical representations of data (like text or images) that capture their semantic meaning. Vector databases are the core technology that powers an agent's long-term **memory** through **RAG**. They function like a librarian who understands the meaning of documents, not just their keywords.

Vector Embeddings - Numerical representations of data (such as words, sentences, or images) that capture their semantic meaning and relationships. Semantically similar concepts will have mathematically close vector embeddings.

Workflow - A sequence of connected, multi-step tasks that collectively accomplish a business objective. The true value of agentic AI is unlocked when it moves beyond automating single tasks to orchestrating entire end-to-end business workflows, such as customer onboarding or issue resolution.

Zero-Trust - A security model based on the principle of "never trust, always verify." It assumes that threats can exist both outside and inside a network, so it requires strict identity verification for every person and device trying to access resources.

Made in the USA
Monee, IL
15 September 2026

63035039R00124